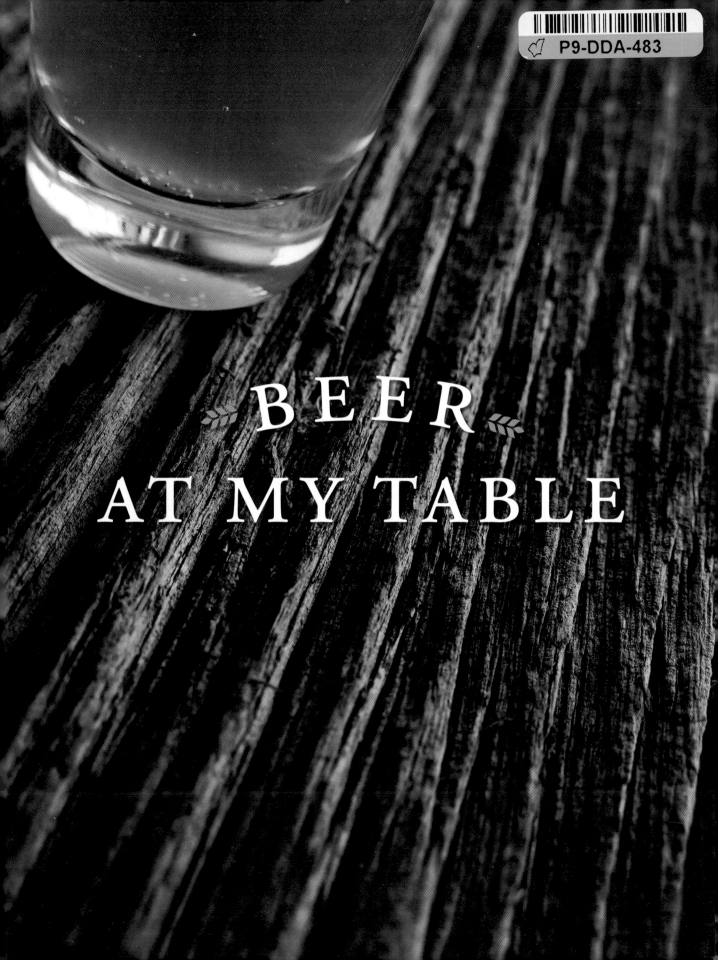

BEER
AT MY TABLE

BEER

AT MY TABLE

RECIPES, BEER STYLES
and FOOD PAIRINGS

Tonia Wilson
CHEF *&* BEER SOMMELIER

Whitecap

Whitecap Books is known for its expertise in the cookbook market, and has produced some of the most innovative and familiar titles found in kitchens across North America. Visit our website at www.whitecap.ca.

EDITOR   Julia Aitken
DESIGN   Andrew Bagatella
FOOD PHOTOGRAPHY   Leonardo Frusteri
PROOFREADER   Barbara Booth

Library and Archives Canada Cataloguing in Publication

Wilson, Tonia, author
Beer at my table : recipes, beer styles and food pairings
/ Tonia Wilson. -- First edition.

Includes index.
ISBN 978-1-77050-318-2 (softcover)

1. Food and beer pairing. 2. Beer tasting. 3. Beer--Flavor
and odor. 4. International cooking. 5. Cookbooks. I. Title.

TP577.W56 2018   641.2'3   C2018-904072-6

We acknowledge the financial support of the Government of Canada through the Canada Book Fund (CBF) for our publishing activities and the Province of British Columbia through the Book Publishing Tax Credit.

Nous reconnaissons l'appui financier du gouvernement du Canada et la province de la Colombie-Britannique par le Book Publishing Tax Credit.

18 19 20 21 22 23   6 5 4 3 2 1

Printed in Canada by Marquis Book Printing

———— ❦ ————

To Tommy,
my loyal confidant, my truthful taste-tester and my love.
Thank you for everything.

To Max and Georgia.
Know that you have a mountain of love beneath your feet
lifting you toward the stars.
May all your dreams come true.

To my family and my girls.
Thank you for a lifetime of wisdom, laughs and love.

———— ❦ ————

CONTENTS

INTRODUCTION

The thought of writing a cookbook had always been in the back of my mind, but it wasn't until I moved to Brussels that the thought became reality. I'd already spent a significant amount of time in Europe, living and working as a chef in the wine countries of France and Italy. But it was my journey to Belgium that opened my eyes to all that beer had to offer.

My appreciation for food had started in France. I was there to finish university, but the most important education I received was how to eat. France changed the way I looked at food and opened my eyes to a world where food was revered. In France, food was prepared with respect and offered with an easy sophistication and grace. From the simplest of goat cheeses to the most elaborate terrines and pastries, the cuisine was infused with a Gallic appreciation of beauty and refinement.

France inspired me to become a chef and after working in restaurants in Canada, I moved to Italy. This is where I really learned to cook. Italy showed me the best food was the simplest, and all that was needed to create a perfect meal were great ingredients, simple preparation and a warm smile. Italy is also where I became a certified wine sommelier and began to really delve into the complexities of aroma, taste and the intricate relationship between what is in the glass and on the plate.

Then I moved to Brussels, discovered Belgium's storied beer culture and everything changed. I had never tasted such interesting beers and there were so many styles to discover. I was enchanted. Belgium opened my eyes to how perfectly beer teamed with food. At first, I felt like I was cheating on wine but as time went on I realized that for many dishes, beer was often the better match.

To Belgians, matching beer with food is innate. They don't talk about it or analyze it, they just do it. Beer is paired with the simplest of offerings—rustic bread smeared with fromage blanc, for example—but also holds court at some of Belgium's most refined tables.

It is this laid-back approach to hospitality that I want to capture in this book. To show that beer has the same versatility and capacity for sophistication as wine.

What I love most about the cuisines of Europe is that woven through all the flavourful dishes are the threads of history, culture, language and art. This is the same reason I adore the world of beer. It is not just a beverage but a link to the agricultural, economic, political and social history that came before us.

Whether you are already a beer lover or new to this most versatile of beverages, I hope this book provides you with a broader understanding of beer and how well it goes with food. I want, as well, to give you the tools to make your own great beer and food choices.

Of course, the most important—and fun—part of learning about beer and food pairing is tasting, and the most effective way to learn is by eating and drinking. In this book, you'll learn how to properly evaluate beer and decipher key components in the food which you're pairing. The recipes are specially designed to feature certain characteristics which influence pairing, such as acidity or fattiness. I want you to be able to smell, taste and feel the sensations in your mouth, to really be able to acknowledge the interaction of beer with food.

This book is meant to be devoured, so I urge you to cook, eat and drink your way through it and come out on the other side with some great new taste experiences and knowledge. It is an offering from me to you, and I hope that it will bring conviviality and joy to your table.

Enjoy,

Tonia

WHAT MAKES A BEER

Most of the world's quality beers are made with just four ingredients: barley, hops, yeast and water. It's remarkable how combining four simple components can create such a diverse array of products. From lively, bright lagers to complex, mesmerizing ales that demand your attention, and everything in between. By getting to know the role of each of these four ingredients you'll have a better understanding of beer in general, and how it will ultimately affect the food you pair it with.

BARLEY Let's begin with barley. Barley is not the only grain used by brewers to brew beer, but it is the most important, and used throughout the world. Brewers require barley for its high concentration of enzymes which are needed to break down the grain's starches into fermentable sugar. The sugar is needed to create alcohol in the beer, but we'll get to that later.

Some of the other grains that you may find in beer are wheat, rye and oats. These grains add extra flavour, texture and interest to the beer, and are never used on their own but always in conjunction with barley. Some brewers might add rice and corn to reduce production costs or lighten a beer's flavour and/or body. Alternative grains such as sorghum and millet are becoming popular in brewing as the demand for gluten-free beer continues to grow.

Dried grains of barley in their natural state are not able to produce beer but need to go through a process known as malting, which turns the barley into

malted barley (or malt). There are three stages to malting. The first is "steeping," where the grains are soaked in water to rehydrate them. Next is "germination," where the grains are drained of excess water and their embryos begin to germinate and sprout rootlets. After the grains have germinated, the third stage—called "kilning"—begins. Here, the grains are heated in a kiln to dry them and stop germination, and it is in the kiln that the malt's future is decided.

The heat of the kiln roasts the malt, and the amount of roasting it receives significantly affects the colour, flavour and aroma of the finished beer. Let's take the colour, for example. If the malt is destined to make a light-coloured beer, such as a pale lager, the malt will get a light toasting. Should the malt be destined for a dark, opaque stout, then the heat will be higher and the grains will be roasted until they are almost black.

As for the flavour and aroma of the final beer, a lighter-roasted malt will offer up aromas of biscuit, straw and hay. Take the roasting a bit further and the malt provides flavours of toffee, caramel and nuts. Go to the darker end of the roasting spectrum and you end up with espresso beans, burnt sugar and bitter dark chocolate. And, this is just a taste of the potential flavour those little grains of barley have to offer. Miraculous indeed.

WATER Where would we be without water? Since it makes up the largest proportion of what is in the bottle, water is obviously an integral part of beer, and also the carrier of all the delicious flavours the brewer creates. It seems almost too simple to say, but without water we wouldn't have beer. Respect water; we need it forever.

The water used in brewing does not necessarily deliver a lot of perceptible flavour of its own, but what it does contribute are minerals, most importantly calcium and magnesium. These will affect the eventual mouthfeel, texture and perceived flavour of a beer. An important point to remember about water is that it can be hard or soft. Hard water is higher in minerals, and the lower the mineral content, the softer the water becomes. This is not something the consumer needs to worry much about, but the composition of the water available is very important to a brewer.

Many years ago, breweries would be located near sources of water that were ideal for brewing. Two cities that attracted breweries on account of their local spring water were Burton-on-Trent in England, and Pilsen in the Czech Republic. Burton-on-Trent was famous for its hard water, perfect for pale ales, while the city of Pilsen was known for the soft water ideal for the celebrated Czech Pilsner. Look to any of the classical beer-brewing cities in Europe—Dublin, Munich, Vienna—and you'll see a connection between the local water and the growth of the area as a brewing stronghold.

Nowadays the mineral composition of local water is not as relevant because brewers can adjust water profiles to suit their brewing needs. They are able to add minerals to water or, conversely, demineralize it to achieve water that is ideal for the beer they plan to brew.

HOPS Hops are another essential ingredient for brewing, and it's their resinous, papery, cone-like flower buds that are used in beer. The flowers grow on hop bines. Yes, that's bines not vines: bines don't have tendrils like vines do but grow by winding themselves around poles and reaching up to 15 metres (50 feet) tall. Once the hop flowers are ready to harvest from the bines, they can be used in a variety of ways. In a process called wet-hopping, the fresh flowers are added directly to the beer. Alternatively, they are dried then used whole, or processed into pellets which are a convenient and popular way of adding hop character to beer. The pellets are also the best means of achieving consistency of flavour from batch to batch, an important consideration for commercial brewers.

Hops have two distinct roles in the brewing of beer. The first is to provide aroma and flavour. Hop varieties that are prized for their aromatic properties are added at the end of the brewing process in order to maximize their

aromatic effectiveness. It's useful to get familiar with some of the more popular types of aromatic hops and their distinct flavour profiles. Once you understand the personality of a certain type of hop, it will allow you to better guess what is inside the bottle or can, and help you decide what type of food the beer will go with. For example, if a beer label lists Cascade hops you can be sure the beer will have citrus notes. If there is mention of the British hop variety called Fuggle (I love that name!), there will be an earthy aroma.

The second important job of hops is to add bitterness to help balance the sweetness in beer. Without hops, most beers would taste cloying and overly sweet. Typically, hops that are favoured for bittering are added early in the brewing process so they have time to release resins and maximize their bittering properties.

When you see the letters IBU on a label, the abbreviation stands for International Bittering Units and refers to the strength of bitterness in the beer. IBUs can range from as low as five in a German Berliner Weisse to 60 or 70 in an American IPA. Remember that the perception of a beer's bitterness can be influenced by the style and weight of the beer. A light-style beer with 20 IBUs would taste significantly more bitter than a malty, sweet beer with a similar IBU level where the beer's body and sweetness temper the effects of the hops.

One last attribute of this unique plant: hops also act as a natural antibacterial preservative for beer.

YEAST Ah, yeast—my favourite little organism. Yeast has done so much to better the food world: it has brought us beer, it has brought us wine, it has brought us bread. Thank you, yeast, for all you do.

It's interesting to note that, up until 1857, people didn't understand the concept of yeast. Even though it is all around us—even on the pages you have before you—yeast can't be seen with the naked eye. It was Louis Pasteur who discovered the fermentation process and yeast's role in it. Traditionally, fermentation in beer occurred when local ambient yeasts in the environment latched onto the sugars in the wort (the sweet liquid derived from mashing together the malt and water) and spontaneously started the process of fermentation. Within days the liquid would have miraculously turned into beer. Can you imagine the joy?

Nowadays, scientists and brewers understand yeast and how it functions (thank Louis Pasteur for that), so they have been able to harness and cultivate yeast strains with certain characteristics, providing brewers a wealth of options for creativity and a plethora of beers for consumers. This means an American brewer can create a beer that tastes like it's from Germany, or a British brewer can brew one that has the personality of a Belgian beer.

When it comes to brewing, yeast is a real workhorse. For starters, it's what creates the alcohol in beer. Yeast is added near the end of the brewing process, after the malt has turned the water into sweet, flavourful wort, and the hops have added their flavour and bitterness. This is when the yeast begins to work its magic. The yeast gets "pitched" (or added) into the sweet, malty liquid where it begins to consume the sugars. As the yeast happily eats away, two by-products are created: alcohol and CO_2 (carbon dioxide). We now technically have beer.

Another important role that yeast plays is to provide aroma and flavour. There are two main families of brewers' yeast that turn sugar into alcohol: ale yeast and lager yeast. Ale yeast functions best at warmer temperatures and generally does its work at the top of the fermentation tank, while lager yeasts work at cooler temperatures and can be found toiling away at the bottom of the fermentation tank. Hence their other descriptors: respectively, top-fermenting and bottom-fermenting yeast.

Both ale and lager yeasts are part of the Saccharomyces cerevisiae family, and there are many strains of both types. The yeasts affect not only aroma in beer, but also mouthfeel. For example, if a brewer chooses to employ a Bavarian-style ale yeast, he or she would end up with a beer that has lovely aromas of banana and clove, and a medium- to full-bodied texture in the mouth. On the other hand, if a British-style ale yeast is used the eventual aromas would be more reminiscent of apples, pears or perhaps apricots, with a rich, smooth texture to the beer. Yet again, should a Czech-style lager yeast be added, the yeast aroma would be minimal because, by nature, lager yeasts contribute less aroma and flavour than ale yeasts. Their main objective is to produce alcohol, create a crisp, clean and dry beer, and let the malt and hops do all the talking.

A third strain of yeast is Brettanomyces, or "Brett" for short. This yeast is also capable of fermenting (and, in fact, spoiling) beer and contributes a very distinctive aroma and flavour to ales. Brettanomyces plays an important role in some older beer styles, such as lambic and the red and brown ales of Flanders in Belgium. In these beers, Brettanomyces is present naturally in the brewery or aging barrels and spontaneously begins fermentation in the beers in an act completely devoid of man's influence and overseen, instead, by Mother Nature. This is considered "spontaneous fermentation" from wild yeast.

Nowadays, Brettanomyces can be purchased and added to beers, making the beers a bit less wild while still retaining the rustic characteristics that Brett provides. Brett has seen a huge resurgence in craft brewing as sour beers have gained in popularity. The aroma and flavour descriptors typically used for beers brewed with Brettanomyces are barnyardy, earthy and funky, as well as tart, dry, sour and lemony. To some, these traits may not sound appealing, but in the skillful hands of the right brewer they can add a complexity and interest to a beer. In a way, these beers are made through controlled spoilage, creating beers that are refreshing, interesting, and a great option for food pairing on account of their higher acid levels.

FRUIT Aside from malt, water, hops and yeast, you may come across other ingredients in beer which are added for complexity and interest. One of the most common is fruit. All sorts of fruit are used to give flavour to beer. Some, such as fruit lambics, have a history behind them, while others—a papaya-enhanced IPA, anyone?—are more contemporary. The chosen fruit can be added in its fresh state after the fermentation process has completed, which helps to retain the fruit's vibrancy. Alternatively, the fruit can be added before fermentation to allow the fruit's sugars to ferment along with those of the wort. This changes the fruit's nature and adds a more complex variation of whatever has been added. Some of the most popular fruits used in brewing are berries, citrus fruit, stone fruit such as plums, cherries and apricots, and, more recently, tropical fruits such as pineapple, passion fruit or mango.

SPICES You may also find beer enhanced with the addition of spices. These can range from baking spices such as cinnamon, cloves or nutmeg (often used in seasonal ales destined to be consumed during holiday time), to ingredients added as a complementary note to the beer in the form of ginger, cumin seeds, grains of paradise or star anise. As long as the beer remains balanced and delicious, the spices that can be used are limited only by the imagination of the brewer.

COFFEE, CHOCOLATE AND MORE For beers with bigger personality and body, the range of potential flavour additions gets even larger. The weight of porters and stouts can withstand the addition of big flavours, and their notes of chocolate and coffee allow them to match with a variety of ingredients. You may find the addition of espresso, milk chocolate or caramel, for example, or even peanut butter, nuts, coconut, hot sauce or vanilla beans, depending on the whim of the brewer.

SWEETENERS Sweet ingredients like brown sugar, honey or maple syrup can be used during brewing to provide different flavour notes. Or, the brewer might add a sweetener to increase the beer's alcohol level while retaining a lighter body. This is a practice commonly used in Belgium when brewing stronger beers, where brewers add a product called "candi sugar," a caramelized sugar product derived from beets. During the fermentation process the yeast not only converts the malt sugars into alcohol but also the candi sugar, increasing the final alcohol level of the beer.

Sugars derived from corn and rice can also be added to beer. This is usually done when brewing mass-market lagers to create light-bodied, low-alcohol and easy to drink beers with low production costs. It is not a practice found in quality beer production but needs to be mentioned as lagers made this way constitute a huge percentage of the beers in the market.

SOUR ALES With the increasing popularity of sour beers, it's useful to know about the bacteria that sour them. There are two types found in sour beers: lactobacillus and pediococcus. Historically, these bacteria would have developed naturally in beers because of lack of refrigeration, the environment, and existing bacteria in the barrels used to store beer. These bacteria consume sugars in the wort and create lactic acid, which gives sour beer its clean, yoghurt-like acidity. The well-loved beer styles of Flanders red and lambic (soured by pediococcus) and Berliner weisse and Gose (soured by lactobacillus) are examples of sour beers that developed naturally. Nowadays, brewers can purchase these bacteria and add them to their beers during production, while more adventurous brewers still allow Mother Nature to do the work.

PAIRING BEER AND FOOD

The best pairing of beer and food is the one that makes you smile and tastes good to you. So, if the enjoyment of eating and drinking is purely subjective and personal, why bother to properly pair beer and food in the first place?

When I teach pairing classes, I'll often start by offering a simple example of a successful pairing to demonstrate why it matters. I'll tell the class to imagine biting into a warm chocolate chip cookie, then taking a sip of cold milk straight from the fridge. Delicious! Pretty much everyone can appreciate the success of this combo. Then I say, imagine taking a bite from that same warm cookie, followed by a sip of thick, sweet mango juice. Hmm, not quite the same warm and fuzzy feeling; the milk makes for a much more enjoyable experience.

This example demonstrates one of the reasons to strive for successful pairings: to get the most enjoyment possible from what we consume. At the very least we are trying to avoid an unpleasant experience; at best, we are looking for a balanced and harmonious combination of flavours that elevate the whole meal.

Another of the main goals in pairing is to choose a beer that has the appropriate amount of bitterness, acidity and/or carbonation to refresh and cleanse the palate after each mouthful of food. Resetting the palate, if you like, for the next bite. Ideally, you take a bite of food, chew and swallow, then take a sip of beer to cleanse the palate while adding complementary flavours to the mouth. This may sound very theoretical; in practice it is a whole lot more fun.

We also seek to enhance the dining experience through successful pairings. We know that wine has long been used to elevate meals, but humble beer never garnered the same esteem. Beer and food pairing is a concept that has only gained serious traction over the last decade or so. While beer has always been on the dinner tables of countries where grains grow better than grapes—England, Belgium and Germany, for instance—elsewhere beer was never really held in the same regard as wine. That has all changed.

The world is smaller now. We have access to beers from all over the world, and craft brewers are constantly offering new and exciting beers to try. As interest in food and cooking has exploded, so has interest in pairing beer with food. Some beers are bold and wacky; some are complex and finessed. But all beers can be served with food to create amazing taste experiences, making dining even more memorable and convivial.

To create a successful beer and food pairing you need to have a good understanding of both sides of the partnership. There are different factors that will affect the pairing in either a positive or negative way. Sometimes you'll already know what food you'll be eating, so you need to think of a complementary beer. Other times you may have a special beer you want to showcase and need to choose food to go with it. Either way, it's important to be aware of the various components of both food and beer. Certainly, there are times—enjoying a pint with some nachos, or a beer and sausage on the dock—when we don't need to overthink what we're consuming. But for the moments that are a little more special, you'll find all the information you need in this book.

THE IMPORTANCE OF BEER STYLES

If you've ever read about beer, you'll have come across the term "beer style." What does it mean? It's fairly self-explanatory: a style of beer. However, there are many, many styles of beer in the world and some may overlap, which can make things a bit confusing.

The term "beer style" was coined and popularized by the late, great beer writer Michael Jackson. He wanted to assign a name to certain styles of beers he'd been tasting throughout his travels. These classifications were very useful in helping to categorize and differentiate between the world's array of beers. Over time, these original style descriptors started being used by the beer-judging communities in the US. They expanded on what Jackson had already created and began using these style descriptors as the criteria upon which homebrew submissions are judged. Homebrewers submit their beers into specific style categories, which are then judged based on how similar they are to the traditional style of the beer. For example, if a brewer submits a Belgian witbier it needs to have the traditional characteristics of refreshing tartness, and aromas of coriander and orange.

Guidelines also stipulate requirements concerning appearance, ingredients, production, aroma and flavour. Beer enthusiasts and home brewers commonly refer to the Beer Style Guidelines set out by the BJCP (Beer Judge Certification Program) in order to confirm the distinguishing traits of a beer style. It is a quick and concise reference catalogue of all the different beer styles of the world.

However, the world of beer continues to evolve, and the landscape has changed immensely. There are always new beers and beer styles coming to market. The craft beer industry has expanded the choice available to consumers. To think that only a few decades ago when someone bought beer, they'd likely be choosing from a small handful of brands, and those were most likely pale lagers. Now the options are almost limitless, which makes it all the more important to understand the styles in order to get full enjoyment. There's no point buying an imperial IPA if you don't enjoy hops. Get the picture?

Craft breweries are smaller and do not have the bureaucratic constraints of large companies, but they're not tied to a historical obligation either, as a centuries-old brewery might be. They can readily and frequently change up their offerings to follow trends and satisfy customers' tastes. This freedom has resulted in countless variations on all the world's beer styles.

Craft brewers continue their quest for inventive, unique brews. The craft consumer's eager appetite for all that is new and different means there are a lot of beers that hit the market that don't fit neatly into any category. And, a lot of the traditional and historical styles are now being tweaked to render them more interesting.

All of it can be a bit confusing if you don't have a basic understanding of the classic styles. One of the objectives of this book is to teach you about the characteristics of some of the most important and popular beer styles of the world. I've chosen a variety of styles. Some are modern classics, such as the American IPA, while others are traditional styles from regions with deep brewing histories, such as Gose or Flanders red. As long as you enjoy what's in your glass, its style name doesn't really matter. But when you're looking to thoughtfully pair beer with food, knowing the personality of the beer will go a long way in helping you choose the right one.

As a chef, I've always believed that to be great at your craft you need to have a strong understanding of the fundamentals of classic cooking techniques, whether they be Chinese, French or Japanese. You need to understand where dishes come from and be able to prepare the classic dishes before starting to go hog wild and take creative liberties. The creative part won't work if you don't have the basic skill set. I feel it is the same with beer, for both consumer and brewer.

Maybe it's just me, but I want to know what a classic Hefeweizen from Bavaria tastes like, before I try a version with Cascade hops and mango added to it. Call me old-fashioned, but I know there are a few of you out there who will catch my drift. That is not to say I won't enjoy the new rendition—I'll probably love it—but I'll appreciate it more if I understand what the original tastes like.

There are two reasons why it is helpful to understand beer styles. The first is so you know what you're buying. And second, so you know what to expect from the beer when you pair it with food. And that is what this book is all about. I'll teach you what you need to know and give you the confidence to create successful beer and food pairings.

Let's start tasting!

THE BEER

Most of us know how to drink beer, and can usually offer up a few adjectives to describe it. But to create confident pairings you'll need to be able to decipher the distinct parts of a beer, put a name to them and know what kind of food makes sense with them or, conversely, which foods should be avoided.

In this chapter, you'll learn how to do an informal evaluation of beer, including its look and aroma, flavour and intensity. In professional terms, the three parts to evaluating a beer are the visual, olfactory and gustatory analysis. This simply means we're going to look at, smell and taste the beer and acknowledge its various characteristics. Part of being able to do this successfully is to develop the vocabulary used in beer tasting, something that will become easier the more beer you taste. I'll start you off with some of the most common adjectives to help lead you down the right path.

A good way to gain confidence in recognizing different aromas and flavours is to always be smelling what is around you, especially anything food-related. Whenever possible take a sniff of cooking ingredients, such as fresh herbs and spices, or breathe in the aromas of bread and pastries coming from your local bakery. You'll eventually come across some of the same aromas in beer. At the very least, it's a pleasant experience and will make you more in tune with your senses, something often lost in a world of overstimulation.

VISUAL ANALYSIS

When we look at a beer it gives us some insight into what is to come. Just as we eat with our eyes first, so do we drink with them. If a beer has a beautiful, rich mahogany colour and a creamy dense head of foam it will look much more appealing than a murky beer with no head and few bubbles. It's easy to understand the importance of a beer needing to appear appetizing as it sends a signal to the brain that there is something pleasant awaiting our taste buds. Next we want to investigate the carbonation, clarity and colour of the beer.

CARBONATION The appearance of the beer's carbonation can give some insight into what you're about to drink, and is the start to understanding the beer's personality. You'll want to make note of the head first to get a proper

read on how long it lasts. Notice the texture and colour of the head. Are the bubbles dense and compact or light and frothy? One of the benefits of foam is that it releases more of the aroma from the glass. If there is little or no head then the beer may be flat from loss of carbonation or in a less-than-clean glass.

Notice the quantity and personality of bubbles in the beer. Are they lively and active or slow-moving? This will tell you something about the presence and behaviour of CO_2 in the beer, or perhaps the presence of nitrogen if the beer looks exceptionally thick and creamy. If it is overly effervescent when poured it may indicate a Belgian-style beer or a bottle-conditioned beer. If there is very little effervescence it could be a cask-conditioned ale.

Once you're partway through the glass, take note of the lacing. This is the residual foam left behind on the inside of the glass. It is considered a sign of quality and also visually pleasing.

CLARITY When examining the clarity of the beer, notice whether the beer has been filtered, in which case it should be transparent and free of particles. If the beer is cloudy or hazy, it is less filtered and still has yeast particles suspended in the liquid. Haziness in beer can be considered a positive thing if it is intentional, as with bottle-conditioned beers where their bubbles are created through a second fermentation in the bottle, leaving the yeast sediment in the beer. Or it can be a brewing defect if the haze is unintentional.

COLOUR The varying colours of beer are a true delight. I still find it amazing how the toasting of a grain of barley can offer such a variety of hues in the finished beer. The colour spectrum for beer ranges from pale straw or light gold through the mid-range colours of amber and copper to brown and black. In addition, there are many variations on all of these. For example, is the beer light or dark copper? It may be an American pale ale. Is it black and opaque? It's likely to be a stout. Or maybe the beer is a kriek or has hibiscus in it and has taken on a dark salmon or rosé hue.

The colour of a beer is usually dictated by the style in which it is brewed. The colour will also offer an indication of its aroma, as well as an idea of taste and weight. For example, a lighter-coloured beer will usually have a lighter taste and weight, while a darker, richer-looking beer will have a weightier mouthfeel, but there are exceptions. For instance, schwarzbiers, dark lagers or Irish stouts look dark and heavy but are instead refreshing and relatively light in alcohol and weight. Conversely, a Belgian tripel is light in colour but has lots of flavour, alcohol and body.

OLFACTORY ANALYSIS

Because our taste buds can detect only six basic sensations—sweet, bitter, sour/acid, salt, savoury/umami and fat—the enjoyment we get from drinking beer relies heavily on its aromas. You can prove this by having a sip of beer while plugging your nose. You will mostly detect tactile sensations in the mouth but very little scent. Unplug your nose to reveal all the wonderful aromas the beer has to offer.

When we take a sip of beer, its volatile aromatic compounds are sent up the back of the throat and into our nasal cavity, where all the action happens. The olfactory receptors can detect more than 10,000 different scents which are relayed to the area of the brain that also regulates our memory. This is why scent is considered to be the strongest trigger of memories. Have you ever smelt something that sent you back in time to, say, the smell of your grandfather's pipe tobacco, your mother's perfume or the waft of a lilac bush in spring? The herbaceous smell of a tomato plant stem always takes me back to my Nan's garden where I'm lying in the grass eating the few cherry tomatoes still hanging on the plant. Scent is an incredibly significant part of our personal history and something to be treasured.

When we are smelling beer there are some specific aromas we are trying to detect, like those relevant to the beer's malt, hops and yeast, as well as any other ingredients, such as fruit or spices.

The first smell that you take of what is in your glass is simply to detect whether the beer is healthy and you find the aroma pleasing. Beers that are unhealthy—or faulty—may have aromas indicating there is something wrong with the beer. The beer may smell "skunky" from prolonged contact with light, or like wet cardboard if it is oxidized, or it may smell of sulphur (or rotten eggs) because of undesirable brewing issues. These are a few of the most common and easily detected faults, but let's concern ourselves with the more positive aromas of beer.

MALT First, you want to think about the malt and its aromas. Do they remind you of toasted bread or biscuits? Or are they darker and deeper, similar to charring from the grill or the scent of roasted espresso beans? The malt may even smell smoky if it has been smoked, or have caramel notes if the brewer has brewed the beer with crystal malt, a specialty malt whose internal sugars have been caramelized.

It's helpful to become familiar with the families of aromas that malt can offer. Some of these are:

- TOASTED NOTES: roasted coffee, dark chocolate or cocoa
- BREADY NOTES: toasted bread, arrowroot cookies, graham crackers or lightly baked biscotti
- SMOKED NOTES: hickory, smoked meat or campfire smoke
- NUT AND DRIED FRUIT NOTES: hazelnuts, pecans, dried apricot, raisins or orange marmalade
- CARAMELIZED NOTES: caramel, burnt sugar, butterscotch, brown sugar, honey, molasses or toffee

HOPS Although its medley of smells won't arrive at your nose in an orderly fashion, try to decipher the beer's aromas step-by-step. It will be less confusing and more effective done this way. Next you'll want to acknowledge the hop aromas. Each variety of hops will provide a different aroma to the beer. Some varieties are quite obvious, while others may be more subtle and harder to pinpoint. Also, some Belgian beers use aged hops which offer almost no aroma.

Some of the common aromas that you'll detect from hops are:

- CITRUS: white or pink grapefruit, lemon, tangerine or orange
- TROPICAL: papaya, gooseberry, mango, pineapple or passion fruit
- FLORAL: rose, lavender, geranium or acacia
- HERBAL: black or green tea, or fresh herbs such as mint, lemongrass or thyme
- RESINOUS: pine, cedar or sap
- STONE FRUIT: peach, apricot, or nectarine
- EARTHY: mushroom, undergrowth, woody, stemmy or leather
- GRASSY: fresh-cut grass, hay, straw, dried herbs or tomato stem

YEAST Yeast is a very special ingredient in beer-making as fermentation cannot happen without it. However, it's not the yeast itself that adds aroma to the beer but the chemical by-products created through fermentation. Simply put, the yeast consumes the wort's sugar and transforms it into alcohol and CO_2, along with volatile aromas called esters and phenols (see page 8 for more on yeast). These aromas are generally fruity and sometimes spicy and occur when warm fermentation temperatures are used, which is why warm-fermented ales are fruitier and more aromatic than cold-fermented lagers.

The aromas will also differ depending on the strain of yeast used. If a traditional German hefeweizen yeast is used, the beer will display aromas of

banana or clove, while a British strain of yeast will result in aromas of pear or apple, and beer brewed with Brettanomyces yeast will have a variety of earthy, funky barnyard aromas.

GUSTATORY ANALYSIS

Here is where we delve into the taste of beer and the tactile sensations perceived in the mouth. While tasting your beer, think about how you perceive the following six tastes and consider the intensity of each. Note that "taste" involves the tactile sensations detected on the tongue, while "flavour" refers to the combination of taste and aroma.

SWEET Sweetness in beer comes from the sugars that are released from the malt. Depending on the beer style, the sweetness level may be quite dry (meaning little or no sweetness) to quite sweet. The "attenuation" of a beer quantifies the final amount of residual sugar left unfermented in the beer. Sugars in a well-attenuated beer have all been fermented into alcohol and carbon dioxide whereas a less-attenuated beer will contain some sweetness from unfermented sugar. A well-balanced beer is one whose sweetness is thoughtfully balanced by the bitterness of hops or roasted malts.

Other ingredients that sweeten beer are brown sugar, maple syrup, honey or fruit. Some examples of styles of beers that have sweetness are Scotch ales, doppelbocks, eisbocks, quadrupels, barley wines and sweet versions of imperial or milk stouts.

When evaluating the sweetness in a beer, consider just how sweet it is. On a scale of dry to cloying, is it moderately sweet or very sweet? Is the sweetness balanced or not? Does it have a similarity to toffee, or brown sugar or milk chocolate? Is there a complete lack of sweetness, as in the case of, say, a sour ale? All of these characteristics will eventually help point you toward the right food for the beer.

BITTER Bitterness in beer comes primarily from the use of hops. The acids derived from the hops give the beer its pleasant bitterness, but also its structure, providing the assertiveness needed to stand up to more substantial and robust foods. The hops also offer the astringency needed to cut through rich, dense foods or dishes with unctuous or fatty sauces.

A second contributor of bitterness is the presence of dark roasted malts, such as those used in brewing porter and stout. Roasted malt tastes bitter—similar to roasted coffee beans—and this acts in the same way as hops to help cleanse the palate. Along with carbonation and acidity, bitterness is one of the three most important traits in beer that make it such an excellent partner for food.

When evaluating the bitterness of a beer, consider how astringent it is. Can you feel the inside of your mouth physically react to the hops or roasted malt, or is it barely noticeable? Think about how intense and persistent the bitterness is. Does the bitterness start in the middle of the tasting experience and continue through to the end, or is there only astringency after you've swallowed?

Examples of styles of beers that have bitterness are European-style pilsners, IPAs, pale ales, hop-forward amber and brown ales, and dry stouts.

SOUR/ACID Acidity is present in all beers, but really becomes detectable in sour ales. Beers that have been intentionally or spontaneously soured have an acidity that other beers do not. This refreshing tartness makes them exceptional at pairing with food, as the acidity makes the mouth salivate, which in turn rinses the palate clean getting it ready for the next bite of food.

When evaluating the acidity in a beer consider how sour or tart it is. Is it mildly tart or intensely acidic? Is the acidity persistent? Is it harsh or soft? Is the acidity lemony and yoghurt-like or more akin to green apple skins?

Some styles of beers that have varying amounts of acidity are witbiers, saisons, gueuzes, American sour and wild ales, Berliner Weisses, Flanders sour ales and some fruit beers.

SALT Saltiness in beer will only be detectable in a beer style such as Gose. It may be present in other beers, depending on the salinity of the water used in brewing, but only in trace amounts that most people would not be able to taste. Saltiness can also be perceived when a salty ingredient has been added to bring a unique flavour to the beer, as in salted black licorice stout or salted caramel stout.

Evaluating saltiness in a beer is simple. How salty is it? Is it the dominant taste or simply mild? Is it intense and persistent?

SAVOURY/UMAMI Savouriness, otherwise known as umami, is the fifth taste. We'll explore it in more depth in the next chapter when we look at its role in food. However, it does show up in some beers, such as darker beers made with roasted malt or beers that have been slightly aged. It is not a common taste but when present in beer can be reminiscent of soy sauce, roasted meat, dried porcini mushrooms or sundried tomato. Beers that may show signs of umami savouriness are stouts and porters, barley wines, and Belgian quadrupels or dubbels.

FAT Fat is the most recently acknowledged taste by scientists who determined that our mouths have a unique taste receptor that detects and reacts to it. Fat does not come into play with beer but is an important consideration in food.

OTHER FACTORS TO CONSIDER

FLAVOUR INTENSITY This is an important consideration when tasting a beer because it will dictate what type of food will pair well. The intensity speaks to the beer's level of boldness or subtlety in terms of aroma, flavour, taste, carbonation and alcohol. Simply put, it refers to the overall personality of the beer. With that decided, you can choose a food that has a similar intensity, whether that be subtle and mild or robust and bold.

ALCOHOL The alcohol level of a beer is one of the factors that gives mouthfeel. Alcohol is viscous (or thick) and coats the inside of the mouth to give a perceived roundness to a beer. You will recognize alcohol in a beer by the warming sensation it gives in the throat. Typically, the higher the alcohol, the fuller-bodied the beer. The round, viscous nature of alcohol can sometimes be perceived as sweetness in a beer, even if it is completely dry. And the presence of elevated alcohol levels can also accentuate the sweetness, piquancy or bitterness in food.

CARBONATION Carbonation—or effervescence—is another mouthfeel factor. It is also beer's secret weapon for food pairing. As it prickles and stimulates the inside of the mouth, it not only makes beer refreshing and lively but acts as a super-efficient palate cleanser, scrubbing away residual grease

or sauciness. Also, the taste of carbonation (CO_2) itself has been scientifically proven to be sour. Which means that along with the bubbles comes acidity to assist in stimulating salivary glands which help to rinse the palate. When tasting the beer, consider the intensity of the carbonation and how long it lasts. Also think about the mouthfeel the carbonation provides: is it frothy and lively, or smooth and creamy?

WEIGHT The weight of a beer is determined by how we perceive its lightness or richness in the mouth. This is similar to intensity but refers only to the heaviness in the mouth. Components of beer that can make it seem heavier are high alcohol levels, the use of oats in the grain bill (the list of grains used in a recipe), or residual sugars that have not been fermented. When pairing beer and food, always try to choose those of similar weight so that one does not overwhelm the other.

THE FOOD

When evaluating a dish of food, the considerations are much like those of beer, but there are many more flavours involved which means more components to acknowledge. Here is what to look for:

VISUAL ANALYSIS

The appearance and presentation of the dish will give you a sense of whether it is something fresh and bright—an asparagus and tarragon omelette or fresh spring roll with shrimp and mango—or heavy and robust—a braised lamb shank or lentil stew. If the dish is drizzled with sriracha sauce or sprinkled with sliced fresh chilies, it will likely be spicy, while a significant amount of soy sauce could lead you to believe there'll be some salty and savoury (umami) tastes. Additionally, a creamy sauce will have you wanting to consider its persistency and heaviness in your pairing.

These types of visual clues will be your first indicators of the type of beer that might make a good pairing. When looking at the food, whether it is in front of you or just a photo in a cookbook, try to recognize the components that will affect the beer. Here's a list of the main things to search for, but don't forget, these are clues and you won't know for sure until you actually taste the food.

- FATS, CREAMS OR OILS: these will be indicators of potential heaviness
- THE INGREDIENTS AND COOKING METHOD: is the dish a light, delicate poached fish or a big, gutsy porterhouse steak with Stilton cheese?
- PIQUANCY (OR CHILI/PEPPERY HEAT): does the dish incorporate spicy ingredients?
- FLAVOUR INTENSITY: does the dish look as if there is a lot or little flavour?
- ACIDITY: are there acidic ingredients, such as tomatoes, or is the dish dressed with sour ingredients, such as lemon or pomegranate seeds?
- SALTINESS: are there salty ingredients, such as soy sauce, cured meats or brined feta cheese?
- BITTERNESS: are bitter ingredients, such as rapini, radicchio or dandelion greens, the main component of the dish? If they are only a small part of the dish or a side dish, they become less relevant to the beer pairing.
- SWEETNESS: are sweet ingredients, such as honey, maple syrup, ripe or dried fruits or chocolate, part of the dish?

OLFACTORY ANALYSIS

The aroma of the food is not the major factor in pairing, but it is relevant. You'll want to consider the intensity of the aroma since, if the food is exceptionally aromatic, you may choose a beer that is more aromatically neutral to let the food do the talking. Vietnamese cuisine, for example, uses aromatic ingredients like mint, basil, cilantro, ginger, lime and green onions, and a pale lager is a great pairing because its subtle aroma doesn't compete with the food.

A different, yet equally successful approach would be to pair Vietnamese food with a beer that complements its herbal nature, such as the lemony brightness of a wheat beer or the bright citrusy notes of an IPA. It all comes down to personal preference.

But imagine for a moment pairing that same bright, fresh food with the intensely dark, roasted coffee notes of a stout and you can see how this would overwhelm the delicacy of the dish. However, the same roasted notes in that stout would work splendidly with a coffee-rubbed roasted leg of lamb, making for a solid flavour link between both food and beer.

GUSTATORY ANALYSIS

SWEET Sweetness in food is typically found in desserts and, when pairing desserts, you'll want to choose beers that also have some sweetness, and a round, soft mouthfeel. Sweet desserts can also be paired well with beers that have a high alcohol percentage. Alcohol's viscosity has the same round, coating thickness as sweetness does, working with the food's sweetness, not against it.

You need to remember that the sweeter the dessert, the sweeter the beer needs to be. Some beers that fall into this category would be barley wines, Scotch ales, doppelbocks, milk stouts, Belgian ales such as quadrupels, and imperial porters and stouts that have some residual sweetness. For desserts that have less sweetness, such as a fruit flan where the fruit's acidity comes into play, you can consider dry fruit beers as a pairing option. Sweeter versions of fruit beers will be great with sweet fruit desserts and those made with chocolate.

It is important to mention that sweetness is not only found in desserts but in many savoury dishes too. Fresh scallops or lobster, rare beef tenderloin and cured meats such as prosciutto all have a sweet tendency. It's also present in buttery cheeses like Saint Agur or triple cream which have the taste of sweet cream. These foods don't necessarily need a sweet beer, but if there is a small amount of residual sweetness in the beer it can make for a really intriguing match, such as the wonderful pairing of a malty, sweet IPA with blue cheese.

BITTER Just as sweet foods call for sweet beers and acidic foods call for tart beers, bitterness in food needs to be paired with a like taste, meaning bitter with bitter. Foods that bring bitterness to a dish are vegetables like radicchio, arugula and rapini, sturdy herbs such as thyme and rosemary, or dried spices like turmeric and cinnamon. Also, the charring or dark caramelizing of foods such as the dark, complex crust on the outside of a slow-cooked roast of beef, can add bitterness. And of course, coffee, cocoa and chocolate all have an intrinsic bitterness.

When pairing beer with bitter choose one that has some bitter qualities coming from either the hops or dark roasted malt or both. Beers to consider are pilsner-style lagers, schwarzbiers, English and American pale ales and IPAs, hop-forward amber and brown ales, and dry porters and stouts.

SOUR/ACID Acidity in food is usually present when an acidic ingredient, such as vinegar, wine or yoghurt, is added or if the dish includes acidic fruits or vegetables, such as tomatoes, pineapple, lemon, limes or pomegranates. Typically, the acidity is tempered with another ingredient to make the complete dish less acidic, which is why we serve, say, a starchy pasta with tomato sauce.

Other examples where acid is present but not necessarily dominant would be dishes served with fermented products such as sauerkraut or kimchi, roast chicken with a lemon-caper sauce, or a zesty fresh salsa on a pulled pork taco. These dishes might have acidity, and you need to consider it, but it's still the chicken and pork that dictate the pairing.

The acidity becomes the dictator when it is the dominant flavour, such as fish marinated in acid, like a ceviche, or a salad where the dressing and any acidic ingredients, such as tomatoes or fruits, will likely dominate the plate.

When acid is at the forefront you want to look to sour beers as your best partner. Of course, sour beers are great with other flavours too, but for acid-based foods, they are ideal. Their acidity helps heighten the flavours, and the acids of both food and beer combine to elevate freshness. Conversely, pairing acidic food with a beer that has malty sweetness would cause the beer to taste off and unpleasant.

SALT Salt is present in almost all foods. It occurs as the natural salinity in seafood, as an inherent ingredient in cheeses, cured salamis and smoked fish or meat, and as a seasoning in the form of basic salt or other salty condiments, such as fish sauce or soy sauce. Salt can be added to a dish to lessen the perception of bitterness or acidity, making those tastes seem softer. An example of this would be a salty farmhouse cheddar paired with an English pale ale, where the salt in the cheese tempers the beer's bitterness allowing the beer's complementary notes of caramel and fruit to really shine. Salt also works as an enhancer of all the other flavours in the dish, which is why unsalted food tastes bland.

SAVOURY/UMAMI It was a Japanese scientist who first discovered our taste buds could detect a fifth taste. The meaty, sapid taste of savoury is often described as "umami," a Japanese word that translates as savouriness. Like salt, umami is an enhancer of other flavours, partly because it is made up of the amino acid called glutamate, the same amino acid found in monosodium glutamate (MSG). MSG is a processed version of glutamate which perhaps is why some people have issues consuming it. However, glutamate in its natural state gives us the pleasing, savoury taste known as umami.

Umami is harder to detect than salty or sweet. Taste sugar or lemon juice and you understand sweet or sour, but umami is not that simple. It is a more complex taste and usually present with other flavours. A great way to isolate and taste umami alone is to roast a piece of beef, then taste some of the cooked browned bits from the bottom of the pan—they are packed with umami.

Umami can be found in a variety of ingredients, but some of the most common are ripe tomatoes (especially the sundried version where flavours are concentrated), mushrooms, asparagus, black olives and eggs. Smoked fish, cured meats, aged cheeses and naturally fermented soy sauce all have an abundance of umami. The savouriness is present in raw meat but becomes intensified when the meat is cooked, especially when roasted or braised.

Savouriness also occurs in fermented or aged foods. Examples of this are miso paste, which is made from fermented soy beans, or aged Parmigiano-Reggiano or Gruyère cheese. Typically, the more the product ages, the more the umami is detectable, which is why a beautiful piece of dry-aged beef is revered for its complex and tasty flavour. For vegetarians, a porcini or shitake mushroom is the best example of the meaty taste of umami, and the dried versions demonstrate it even more.

FAT Fat in food can come from many different sources: from chicken, pork, fatty fish or beef; from butter, lard, cream or oils used in cooking; or from naturally fatty ingredients, such as avocadoes, nuts or seeds. When contemplating the fat content of a dish, consider how much is used and how prevalent it is. Also consider whether the fat is animal-derived, as in butter and beef marbling, or vegetable-derived, as in olive and peanut oil. The fat from animals is more persistent on the palate than fats from vegetables, and may call for a beer with more cleansing power, like one with elevated hopping, or a highly carbonated beer, like a bottle-conditioned ale.

OTHER FACTORS TO CONSIDER

FLAVOUR INTENSITY This is one of the most important dictators of the type of beer you will pair with the food. Your beer choice will be made largely based on the flavour intensity of the dish. Is the food delicate or robust? The intensity of the food speaks to its boldness, or lack thereof. You want to consider the intensity of the flavours, the level of spicing, the fresh herbs used, the amount of searing, and the innate flavour of the ingredients. Take into account anything in the dish that gives it flavour, then evaluate how much of that flavour is present. Is it mild and subtle, or intensely flavoured and bold?

WEIGHT As with beer, the weight of the food is determined by how we perceive its lightness or fullness in the mouth. This is not the same as intensity and refers only to the tactile feeling in the mouth, not the flavours. An example of light food would be cod poached in white wine, while a heavy dish might be braised short ribs. Components of food that usually make it seem heavier are high levels of fat, oil or cream; cooking styles, such as braising, which creates succulence; and ingredients that by nature can create heavier dishes, such as fatty meats, cheeses, and starches such as rice in a risotto. Lighter-weight dishes can, but are not always, created with ingredients such as fish, seafood, vegetables, eggs and broth.

PIQUANCY Piquancy or spiciness in food is derived from using ingredients that have a natural heat, such as jalapeños and other hot peppers, ginger, wasabi, mustard or horseradish. It can also be present when a dish is seasoned with spices or condiments with heat, such as various types of peppercorns, hot sauces, Asian black bean sauce, harissa and chili or curry pastes.

PUTTING IT ALL TOGETHER

Now that we've covered how to properly evaluate the attributes of beer and food, it's easy to start pairing. This is where the fun really happens. Use the information below to start exploring how beer and food interact. And of course, use the recipes that follow to help confirm the knowledge you've already gained. Enjoy the journey of learning as it never really ends. Even unsuccessful pairings will teach you something new. Now, let's get to it!

THE GOALS

1. To create a balanced harmony between beer and food, and elevate both to a more flavourful and pleasing experience.
2. To avoid any unpleasant flavour interactions.
3. To make sure the beer has the ability to clean and refresh the palate.
4. To link any similar or complementary flavours between beer and food.

THE STEPS

STEP ONE: *Evaluate Intensity, Weight and Texture*

EVALUATE THE INTENSITY OF THE FOOD: How aromatic is it? How flavourful? Is it raw or cooked, sauced or not?

CONSIDER THE WEIGHT OF THE FOOD: Is it a light and flaky fish or a succulent pork chop? Is it a dense pound cake or an airy meringue?

Now decide what level of intensity your beer will need to match it. This is where it helps to be familiar with beer styles so you can choose something appropriate.

STEP TWO: *Consider the main taste (not flavour) factors affecting the dish*

What are the tastes that dominate the plate? Fattiness in smoked salmon? Sweetness from a chocolate tart? Saltiness from cheese? Know the dominant taste sensations you'll need to pair.

STEP THREE: *Consider the main flavour (not taste) factors affecting the dish*

What are the main flavours? If there is a protein, consider its flavour but also take into account the other flavours involved. Garlicky aïoli? Smoky barbecue sauce? Herbaceous pesto? Are there exotic spices? It is these flavours you want to link to the flavours in the beer. Some examples of this are herbal notes in the food paired with herbaceous hop aroma, or a pecan tart paired with a nutty beer. How about the dark charring on meat linked with the smokiness of rauchbier? This replaying of flavour can help create a great pairing that makes sense.

STEP FOUR: *Consider what type of beer will cleanse the palate*

Here you will need to consider the weight, persistency and succulence of the dish. Is the dish palate-coating and heavy, or delicate with little fattiness? Heavier, fattier dishes will need more of the cleansing abilities of acidity, bitterness or carbonation. Lighter dishes will need less.

It's important to understand how palate-cleansing actually happens. The three traits in beer that can clean and reset the palate are as easy to remember as your ABCs:

- ACIDITY: acid makes the salivary glands release saliva which acts to rinse the palate clean.
- BITTERNESS: the astringency of bitterness dries off the palate and cuts through the sauciness or heaviness in a dish.
- CARBONATION: the foaming action of the bubbles acts to scrub residual food off the palate.

THE PRINCIPLES

The following guidelines can lead you in the right direction, but until you get everything in your mouth nothing is for sure. As you continue practising and learning you'll start making decisions based on instinct, which most of us already have the ability to do if we relax and have confidence in ourselves. These principles simply help refine things and put words to what you are tasting in your mouth.

If the food's dominant traits are:

- SWEET: pair with a beer that has sweetness, an elevated level of alcohol and/or bitterness
- BITTER: pair with a beer that has a similar level of bitterness, either from hops or roasted malt
- SOUR: pair with a beer that has perceivable acidity, as in sour ales
- SALTY: pair with a beer that has perceivable acidity, a high amount of carbonation and little bitterness
- FATTY: pair with a beer that has bitterness, perceivable acidity and/or a high amount of carbonation
- SPICY: pair with a malt-forward beer, preferably one that has some malty sweetness and a lesser level of alcohol, as alcohol only intensifies piquancy
- SAVOURY/UMAMI: umami is not normally the dominant taste in a dish but accompanies a flavour, so choose a beer that is complimentary to the flavour. However, take into consideration that umami can intensify the tastes of sour, sweet and bitter, and accentuate the heat of alcohol. Most often the beers that will accompany umami have a high flavour intensity.

THE RECIPES

Now the fun begins. Take all the information you've learned and use it to further enjoy the beer and food you consume. Some of your pairings will be stellar, some will be mediocre. It doesn't matter as long as you're enjoying yourself.

We are so fortunate to have access to a world full of wonderful products created by skilled brewers, food makers and farmers. Let's cook, sip, eat and share it all with the people we love. I hope you enjoy the rest of this book The recipes I've created are seasonal and include ingredients that shouldn't be too hard to find. Some are quick and easy, others may take a bit more time, but they're all designed to showcase the principles of food and beer pairing outlined in the previous chapters.

So, roll up your sleeves, pour yourself a glass of beer, dive in and enjoy yourself.

SPRING

BELGIAN WITBIER 48
Tartine of Smoked Trout with Herbed Cheese and Radishes 50

CALIFORNIA COMMON 52
Thai Red Curry Mussels with Coconut Milk 54

TRAPPIST ALE 56
Steak Tartare with Charred Peppers and Lemon-Chive Mayonnaise 58

GUEUZE 60
Artichoke, Pea and Lemon Carbonara 62

VIENNA LAGER 64
Pomegranate-Glazed Lamb Meatballs with Green Pea Hummus 66

AMERICAN PALE ALE 68
Roasted Cod with Mango Pickle 70

CZECH PILSNER 72
Chicken Schnitzel with Apricot, Gruyère and Arugula Salad 74

DOPPELBOCK 76
Rack of Lamb with Pistachio-Dijon Crust 78

AMBER ALE 80
Beef Tenderloin with Béarnaise Aïoli 82

Belgian Witbier

{ TARTINE *of* SMOKED TROUT *with* HERBED CHEESE *and* RADISHES }

Witbier (white beer in English or *bière blanche* in French) is a Belgian ale brewed from wheat as well as malted barley. Both malted and unmalted wheat are used in varying percentages, depending on the brewer. The wheat and unfiltered yeast in witbier give the beer its cloudy appearance and pale colour, and also great head retention (which is why brewers will sometimes add a small amount of wheat to a beer that doesn't traditionally contain it).

Witbiers are designed to be drunk fresh and young, and are known for their refreshing nature, bright personality and simple elegance. Expect to smell aromas of citrus and spice coming from the addition of orange peel and coriander seed, as well as some pepperiness from the Belgian yeast.

The grain aroma is primarily of wheat which helps add to the bright, brisk personality of the beer. Hops are not really part of the discussion here since they are used only to add a small amount of bitterness rather than aroma or flavour.

Its elevated level of carbonation—lots of fine, effervescent bubbles—makes Belgian witbier the perfect foil for any food that's fatty, oily or saucy.

PAIRING: *Blanche de Chambly, Unibroue (Canada)*

Blanche de Chambly is brewed in the classic Belgian style, so you'll notice its dense white head and hazy appearance. The beer has a light, creamy mouthfeel which won't overwhelm the delicacy of the tartine. Its lemony, citrus notes complement the trout perfectly, and its effervescence helps cleanse the palate of the richness of both the fish and the cream cheese. Look for additional aromas of coriander, spearmint and white pepper in each sip, which echo the herb and pepper garnish of the tartine.

OTHERS TO TRY:

Allagash White, Allagash Brewing Company (USA)
Hoegaarden Witbier (Belgium)
White Ale, Hitachino Nest Beer (Japan)

{ BELGIAN WITBIER }

Tartine *of* Smoked Trout *with* Herbed Cheese *and* Radishes

The scattering of radishes on these open-face sandwiches is a nod to a classic spring snack popular in Belgium: radishes on buttered toast with sea salt.

1 cup (250 mL) good-quality cream cheese, at room temperature

2 Tbsp (30 mL) thinly sliced chives

2 Tbsp (30 mL) finely chopped dill

1 tsp (5 mL) finely grated lemon zest (use a rasp for best results)

2 Tbsp (30 mL) salted butter, softened

8 slices light rye bread

6 oz (175 g) boneless, skinless smoked trout fillet, broken into pieces

6 small radishes, trimmed and very thinly sliced

Salt and freshly ground black pepper to taste

Chives and/or dill sprigs for garnish

1. Adjust the oven rack to the middle position and preheat the broiler to high.

2. In a medium bowl, stir together the cream cheese, chives, dill and lemon zest until well combined.

3. Butter one side of each slice of bread. Place the slices, buttered side up, on a baking sheet. Place the baking sheet on the middle rack of the oven and broil until the bread is lightly golden, about 2 minutes.

4. Spread the toasted bread generously with the cheese mixture, then top with the trout and radishes, dividing evenly. Season with salt and pepper to taste. Garnish with herbs, then serve.

Serves 4

California Common

{ THAI RED CURRY MUSSELS *with* COCONUT MILK }

California Common is part of a family of beers considered to be hybrids, which mean they combine elements of both a lager and an ale. The style known as California Common originated in San Francisco on account of circumstance and climate. The short story is that brewers who arrived in California for the gold rush in the 1840s had with them only lager yeasts. These yeasts work best at cooler temperatures but there was no refrigeration nor ice. So their beers were left to ferment at ambient temperatures more suited to ale yeasts, creating beers with an ale's mild fruitiness.

Of the four hybrids, California Common is the only one that uses lager yeasts at ale temperatures. The other three—Germany's Kölsch (from Cologne), altbier (from Dusseldorf) and North American cream ale—are fermented with ale yeasts at cold lager temperatures. While Kölsch and altbier are both beers of balance, subtle aroma and a clean, dry personality, altbier is brewed with a darker malt which amps up the colour, body and flavour, and adds a touch of bitterness. Cream ale is a light, dry, highly carbonated beer with an even balance between the flavours and aromas of malt and hops. It is a very "sessionable" beer, meaning it's an easy drinking beer with lower alcohol so you can enjoy several, and a flavourful option if you are looking for something with more body than a regular pale lager.

California Common beers have a fuller mouthfeel than a lager but retain a lager's smooth, clean crispness. They also have a fairly assertive hop personality from the use of classic American hop varieties, most commonly Northern Brewer.

PAIRING: *Anchor Steam, Anchor Brewing (USA)*

First a bit of history. California Common beers were once referred to as steam beers, so named, some say, for the steam which drifted from the surface of the cooling wort. The beers had their heyday during the California gold rush but eventually fell out of favour. In 1971, San Francisco's Anchor Brewing Company resurrected the style with the release of its Steam Beer. By the time its competitors got around to brewing in this style, Anchor Brewing Co. had already trademarked the name, forcing all other breweries to refer to their versions as California Common.

Anchor Steam has aromas of sweet malt, caramel and earthy hops. The noticeable bitterness in the beer stretches from the beginning to the end, and finishes clean and dry with a residual taste of dried herbs and tobacco leaf. When considering a pairing for the beer I wanted a dish that made sense on a textural level. The hopping of this beer is assertive and needs to be considered. What would be a good contrast for bitter? Silkiness, of course, which is just what the coconut milk-laced broth delivers in the mussel dish. While the mussels bring salinity and minerality into the equation, they are mild-tasting so it is the sauce's personality that must be given the most consideration. The heat from the red curry paste and chili pepper needs to be tempered and this is where the beer's sweet malty backbone works perfectly to gently balance the spice. In addition, the pops of bright flavour and aroma from the lime, cilantro and green onions add to a pairing that works wonderfully.

OTHERS TO TRY:
Gaffel Kölsch (Germany)
Track 85 Lagered Ale, Old Tomorrow (Altbier/ Canada)
Calm Before the Storm, Ballast Point (Cream Ale/USA)

{ CALIFORNIA COMMON }

Thai Red Curry Mussels *with* Coconut Milk

*Different brands of red curry paste have different intensities so you may need
to add more if you like your mussels with a bit of a kick. As for the beer, use the same
one you're planning to serve with the mussels.*

3 lb (1.5 kg) mussels

3 Tbsp (45 mL) unsalted butter

2 Tbsp (30 mL) finely
chopped garlic

½ tsp (2 mL) finely
chopped seeded red chili
pepper (or to taste)

1 Tbsp (15 mL) red curry
paste (or to taste)

1½ cups (375 mL) beer
(see note above)

1 cup (250 mL) coconut milk

½ cup (125 mL) finely sliced
green onions

1 tsp (5 mL) finely
grated lime zest (use a
rasp for best results)

¼ cup (60 mL) coarsely
chopped cilantro

Lime wedges for garnish

Naan-style bread
to serve

1. Scrub the mussels and remove any beards. Discard any mussels that do
not close when tapped on the counter. Set aside.

2. In a large pot, melt the butter over medium heat. Add the garlic and chili
pepper and cook, stirring, until softened, about 5 minutes.

3. Add the red curry paste, stirring to blend it into the garlic mixture. Add
the beer and simmer until it has reduced slightly.

4. Add the coconut milk, green onions and lime zest, then simmer for
3 minutes. Taste and add more red curry paste, if needed.

5. Add the mussels to the pot. Cover the pot and increase heat to medium-high. Cook, stirring occasionally, until the mussels have opened, about
8 minutes. Discard any mussels that do not open.

6. Scatter with the cilantro, garnish with lime wedges and serve at once
with naan-style bread.

Serves 4

Trappist Ale

{ STEAK TARTARE *with* CHARRED PEPPERS *and* LEMON-CHIVE MAYONNAISE }

I've included Trappist Ale here to show that it is a beer category that encompasses different styles, such as quadrupels and dubbels. But in addition, I want to explain the significance of Trappist Ale as a trademark. When a beer is labelled Authentic Trappist Product, it indicates the beer was brewed in accordance with the regulations set out by the International Trappist Association, a group of monks of the Cistercian Order. The trademark guarantees the beer was brewed either by Trappist monks or under their strict supervision within the walls of their monastery, and that proceeds from the beer sales are used for charity and maintenance of the abbey. To a beer drinker, the trademark means there is probably something pretty sensational inside the bottle.

Six of the eleven Trappist breweries are located in Belgium (Orval, Westvleteren, Rochefort, Chimay, Westmalle and Achel), two in the Netherlands (Koningshoeven and De Kievit) and the remaining three are in Austria (Stift Engelszell), Italy (Tre Fontane) and the USA (Spencer). Trappist beers are considered some of the greatest beers in the world and are beloved by many. Throughout the world, there are many secular beers brewed in styles associated with abbeys, but these are called abbey-style ales, not Trappist ales.

Trappist beers have different personalities based on the monastery where they are brewed, but they share some common traits. All Trappist beers are complex, aromatic and flavourful and usually have elevated levels of alcohol. They are typically bottle-conditioned, meaning they will have a fine and abundant effervescence. Depending on the beer's style, you will encounter fruity, herbal or floral aromas enhanced with spice notes of pepper or clove, and possibly complex notes of dried fruit, toffee, nuts, molasses, cocoa and tobacco.

Simply put, Trappist beers are exceptional and exciting, and demand attention for their uniqueness. To learn more about the individual Trappist ale styles, refer to the pairing information for Dubbel (page 182), Tripel (page 174) and Quadrupel (page 132) beer styles, the primary styles brewed by the monasteries.

PAIRING: *Orval, Brasserie d'Orval (Belgium)*

Orval starts with a foundation that is recognizable as a Belgian beer but is then layered with heaps of perfumed aroma and complexity. The initial notes are that of violet, marjoram and green tea. And there is also a funky barnyard

note. Say, what? Well, it smells a bit like a mix of a cow's derrière, straw and damp barn board all mixed together, but in the most elegant of ways. This earthiness comes from the addition during the fermentation process of a yeast strain called Brettanomyces. This adds yeast a layer of complexity to the beer, as well as an acidic tartness you'll notice on the palate. The addition of dry hops near the end of brewing also adds more dimension to the beer, adding a whack of florality and an obvious astringency on the finish.

There are many reasons this beer works so well with the steak tartare. Both beer and steak have a similar mouthfeel. The beer's herbaceous and floral notes are great complementary "garnishes" to the meat, and the cutting nature of the beer's effervescence and bitterness is perfect for contrasting the silky texture of both the steak and the roasted peppers. Lastly, this is one of those psychological pairings, in that the steak and beer both exude Franco-Belgian sophistication and just feel right together.

{ TRAPPIST ALE }

Steak Tartare *with* Charred Peppers *and* Lemon-Chive Mayonnaise

A good, very sharp chef's knife is essential here for dicing the beef into small cubes.

¾ lb (375 g) piece well-trimmed beef tenderloin

1 medium sweet red pepper

½ cup (125 mL) mayonnaise

1 Tbsp (15 mL) finely sliced chives

1 tsp (5 mL) Worcestershire sauce

1 tsp (5 mL) finely grated lemon zest (use a rasp for best results)

1 Tbsp (15 mL) lemon juice

2 Tbsp (30 mL) drained capers, coarsely chopped, plus ½ tsp (2 mL) reserved liquid from caper bottle

2 Tbsp (30 mL) finely chopped red onion

2 Tbsp (30 mL) olive oil

1 tsp (5 mL) your favourite hot sauce (or to taste)

½ tsp (2 mL) salt and freshly ground black pepper

¼ tsp (1 mL) smoked paprika

4 cups (960 mL) lightly packed washed and dried arugula, mâche or watercress

Additional oil for drizzling

Lightly toasted baguette slices to serve

Lemon wedges for garnish

1. Wrap the beef in plastic wrap and freeze for 30 minutes while preparing the other ingredients (this will make it easier to slice).

2. Char the pepper either by holding it with tongs over the flame of a gas burner, grilling it on a hot barbecue, or broiling it, turning often, until blackened on all sides, about 10 minutes. Set the pepper aside to cool slightly.

3. When the pepper is cool enough to handle, peel off the skin, discard the seeds and stem, then finely dice (you should have about ½ cup/125 mL). Put the pepper in a medium bowl and set aside in the refrigerator.

4. In a small bowl, stir together the mayonnaise, chives, Worcestershire sauce, lemon zest and juice. Set aside.

5. Using a very sharp knife, cut the beef into very small cubes, no larger than ¼-inch (6 mm). The easiest way to do this is to cut a few ¼-inch slices. Stack the slices, cut them into ¼-inch strips, then slice the strips into ¼-inch cubes.

6. Add the beef cubes, capers and caper liquid, onion, olive oil, hot sauce, salt, pepper and paprika to the roasted pepper and combine gently. Taste and add more salt and pepper if necessary.

7. Divide the steak tartare among four chilled plates. Add a handful of arugula drizzled with olive oil to each plate, then garnish plates with reserved mayonnaise and lemon wedges. Serve with toasted baguette slices.

Serves 4

Gueuze (or Geuze)

{ ARTICHOKE, PEA *and* LEMON CARBONARA }

Gueuze is a traditional Belgian beer style unique to Brussels. It is a blend of lambic beers which range in age from one to three years.

What is a lambic beer? Simply put—and, really, it's far from simple—lambic beer is created by allowing local, indigenous yeasts and bacteria to inoculate, or attach themselves to, the wort. This happens overnight while the wort is cooling in wide, shallow tanks, called coolships, that allow exposure to air. This type of uncontrolled process is called spontaneous fermentation. The wort is inoculated overnight, then goes into large barrels to await fermentation which can take a few days or even weeks to begin. Once the majority of CO_2 has been released from the barrels, they are plugged (or bunged) and left to develop and age. Wild yeasts and bacteria will slowly continue to ferment and sour the beer during this uncontrolled process which can last from one to three years. Mother Nature is doing all the work here which means each batch of beer will be different and, in a world of consistency and homogenization, this is a rare treat. One of the wild yeasts at work here is Brettanomyces, and tasting gueuze is a good way to experience the funk and barnyard qualities that this yeast can contribute.

Lambic is a still, uncarbonated beer which gains its fine and gentle effervescence through bottle fermentation. The bottles containing a blend of one- to three-year-old lambics are left in bottle for up to one year so they can slowly re-ferment and become effervescent before being released to the eagerly awaiting admirers of the style.

The different ages of lambic beer that go into gueuze contribute different characteristics to the finished beer. The one-year-old lambic adds brightness and residual sugar, and it is the sugar that will eventually ferment into bubbles within the bottle. The two- and three-year-old lambics, that have had time to age and sour in barrels, give complexity and depth. The different lambics are added in specific proportions by a skilled blender who creates the gueuze to be representative of the brewery's style.

Gueuze is something of an acquired taste. I have poured it for people who have been wildly shocked that it tastes so different from other beers. But that is the beauty of this beer. It is exceptionally interesting and offers an opportunity to taste history and get a sense of the terroir of Brussels, one of the world's great beer cities.

PAIRING: *Cuvée René, Brouwerij Lindemans (Belgium)*

Like most gueuzes, this beer has a tart lemony nose with intriguing aromas of funk, and lactic, lemony earthiness reminiscent of a good-quality French chèvre (goat milk cheese) like Crottin de Chavignol.

As for the pairing, the easy part was knowing that the lemon aroma in the beer would complement the lemon zest and artichokes in the pasta dish. The harder part was getting the balance right between the beer and the creamy persistency of the sauce.

The beer is rather low in carbonation, therefore the bubbles help a little in cleansing the palate, but most of the workload goes to the piercing acidity of the beer. This high acidity stimulates the saliva needed to rinse the mouth clean, while at the same time leaving a pleasing bready flavour and, of course, some of the complementary lemon curd notes. As a general rule, I don't tend to suggest beer as a pairing with pasta, but gueuze has more similarities with a sparkling white wine, which is why it works so well with this flavourful and elegant carbonara.

I hope the Romans approve.

OTHERS TO TRY:

Oude Geuze, Brouwerij Oud Beersel (Belgium)
Oude Geuze, Brouwerij 3 Fonteinen (Belgium)
Oude Geuze, Brouwerij Boon (Belgium)

{ GUEUZE }

Artichoke, Pea *and* Lemon Carbonara

Use the freshest eggs you can find for this simple pasta dish as the bright yellow of the yolks adds colour to the sauce. Guanciale is Roman-style cured pork cheek; a good deli should have it.

Salt to taste

¼ cup (60 mL) olive oil

2 Tbsp (30 mL) finely chopped garlic

5 oz (150 g) guanciale or mild pancetta, chopped into ¼-inch (6 mm) dice

1½ cups (375 mL) artichoke hearts, each sliced into eight (drain and rinse if using bottled artichokes)

1¼ cups (310 mL) finely grated Pecorino Romano (about 2½ oz/75 g)

2 large eggs

2 Tbsp (30 mL) finely chopped flat-leaf parsley

2 tsp (10 mL) finely grated lemon zest (use a rasp for best results)

Freshly ground black pepper to taste

1 lb (500 g) good quality dry spaghetti

¾ cup (175 mL) fresh or frozen peas

Additional olive oil for drizzling

Additional finely grated Pecorino Romano for garnish (optional)

1. Bring a large pot of water to the boil over high heat. Add enough salt to the water so you can taste it.

2. Meanwhile, in a medium saucepan heat the oil over low heat. Add the garlic and cook until softened and fragrant, about 3 minutes. Add the guanciale and cook until the fat renders, about 5 minutes. Increase the heat to medium and cook until the guanciale is golden, about 5 more minutes.

3. If using bottled artichokes add them to the saucepan and cook for 2 minutes. If using fresh artichokes, add them to the saucepan along with ½ cup (125 mL) of water, then simmer and cover. Flip artichokes occasionally until they are tender when pierced with a knife, about 20 minutes. Turn off the heat.

4. In a bowl large enough to hold the pasta, whisk together the cheese, eggs, parsley, lemon zest and pepper. Set aside.

5. Add the pasta to the boiling, salted water and cook as per package instructions. If using fresh peas, add them to the pot 3 minutes before the pasta is ready; if using frozen peas, add them to the pot 1 minute before the pasta is ready.

6. Meanwhile, reheat the artichoke mixture over medium heat until the cooking liquid has reduced and the artichokes are golden, about 5 minutes.

7. When the pasta is al dente, scoop out and reserve 1 cup (250 mL) of pasta cooking water from the pot, then drain the pasta. Add the pasta to the cheese mixture and toss well.

8. Add the artichoke mixture to the pasta and toss again until the pasta is well coated with the sauce. The sauce should not be dripping; it may take a minute of tossing and stirring until the liquid from the sauce is absorbed. Conversely, you can add a small amount of the reserved cooking water to loosen the sauce if needed.

9. Serve immediately, drizzling each portion with additional olive oil, and adding a scattering of black pepper and additional cheese, if desired.

Serves 4

Vienna Lager

{ POMEGRANATE-GLAZED LAMB MEATBALLS *with* GREEN PEA HUMMUS }

Vienna lager, an amber beer, is a style originally created in Vienna, Austria in 1841, but it was the advent of pale malt in England that sparked the lager's beginnings. Before the 1840s, beers were made with deeply roasted malt which made them very dark. Two Austrian brewers brought the new and popular pale malt back to Vienna and used it to create what we now know as Vienna lager.

Nowadays the style has more presence outside Europe, and craft brewers have taken to creating delicious versions of the style the world over. It is a well-balanced beer that has great food-pairing capabilities as it is flavourful with a medium mouthfeel, and its caramel bread notes are very compatible with a wide array of foods. No matter where it is brewed, the recipe will always include Vienna malt in its grain bill (the list of grains used in the recipe). This specialty malt adds the characteristic sweet bread crust aroma and rich, toffee-tinged maltiness to the beer. The use of noble hop varieties such as Saaz give pleasant bitterness and earthy aroma, with the hop character prevalent but not overwhelming.

PAIRING: *Boston Lager, Samuel Adams (USA)*

This lamb meatball dish brings a few different components to the plate but the factors that need the most consideration are the sweet and sour pomegranate glaze and the cumin-tinged meatballs. The beer has just the right amount of sweet buckwheat honey maltiness to balance the tang of the pomegranate, and the beer's generous aromatics are a great complement to the lamb's spicing. Pleasing notes of candied orange, toffee and ginger in the beer all go wonderfully with the cumin and coriander.

Lamb can typically be a heavier, fattier meat but when turned into meatballs its weight and texture are lightened which calls for a medium-weight beer with sufficient hopping to cleanse the palate of any residual fat. The secondary components of the dish are the yoghurt and hummus, which both have palate-coating persistency. Once again, the beer's moderate hopping, along with its carbonation, are exactly what's needed to reset the palate. Overall, this pairing works well because of the similar flavour intensities, complementary aromas and a harmonious balance of weight.

OTHERS TO TRY:
Top Shelf Vienna Lager, Lake of Bays Brewing Co. (Canada)
Eliot Ness Amber Lager, Great Lakes Brewing Co. (USA)
Negra Modelo, Grupo Modelo (Mexico)

{ VIENNA LAGER }

Pomegranate-Glazed Lamb Meatballs *with* Green Pea Hummus

1½ lb (750 g) ground lamb

½ cup (125 mL) finely chopped green onions

⅓ cup (80 mL) coarsely chopped cilantro

1 egg

1 Tbsp (15 mL) dried bread crumbs

1 Tbsp (15 mL) ground cumin

2 tsp (10 mL) ground coriander

1½ tsp (7 mL) salt

Pinch of chili flakes (or to taste)

1 cup (250 mL) Greek or other thick yoghurt

3 Tbsp (45 mL) olive oil, divided

2 Tbsp (30 mL) finely chopped mint

1 cup (250 mL) pomegranate juice

2 Tbsp (30 mL) packed brown sugar

1 Tbsp (15 mL) balsamic vinegar

2 mini cucumbers or half an English cucumber, thinly sliced

½ cup (125 mL) pomegranate seeds (optional)

Additional mint for garnish

Green Pea Hummus (recipe follows)

Pita bread to serve

1. In a large bowl, gently mix together the lamb, green onions, cilantro, egg, bread crumbs, cumin, coriander, salt and chili flakes until well blended. Form into 24 even-sized meatballs. Refrigerate until ready to cook.

2. In a small bowl, stir together the yoghurt, 1 Tbsp (15 mL) olive oil, mint and salt to taste. Set aside.

3. In a large skillet, heat the remaining olive oil over medium-high heat. Working in batches, if necessary, add the meatballs to the skillet and cook, turning often, until browned and cooked through, about 15 minutes.

4. When all the meatballs are cooked, drain off any fat from the skillet. Return all the meatballs to the skillet and add the pomegranate juice, brown sugar and balsamic vinegar. Cook over medium-high heat, stirring often, until the liquid thickens into a light syrup consistency and coats the meatballs.

5. Let cool slightly then garnish with the cucumber, pomegranate seeds (if using) and mint. Serve with the yogurt and hummus, with pita bread on the side.

Serves 4

Green Pea Hummus

2 cups (500 mL) fresh or frozen peas

2 cloves garlic, finely sliced

2 Tbsp (30 mL) olive oil

½ tsp (2 mL) ground coriander

½ tsp (2 mL) granulated sugar

½ tsp (2 mL) salt

Your favourite hot sauce to taste

1. In a small saucepan, combine the peas, garlic and just enough water to cover them. Cover and bring to a boil over high heat. Immediately lower the heat and simmer for 3 minutes. Strain, reserving the cooking liquid.

2. Place the peas, garlic, olive oil, coriander, sugar and salt in a food processor or blender. Process until smooth, adding the reserved cooking liquid in small quantities, if needed, to loosen the mixture and allow it to form a purée. Season to taste with hot sauce. Set aside to cool, then refrigerate until ready to serve.

Makes 2 cups (500 mL)

American Pale Ale

{ ROASTED COD *with* MANGO PICKLE }

American Pale Ale (APA) was created in the 1980s when American craft brewers began making beer in the classic British pale ale style. What differentiates these beers from their counterparts across the pond is the use of American ingredients, particularly American hop varieties, such as Cascade, Citra, Centennial, Simcoe and Amarillo. These native hops give APAs their characteristic citrus and pine aromas.

APAs have balanced flavours, bright citrusy aromas and a bitterness that is noticeable but not overwhelming. They are more aromatic and bolder in flavour than their more traditional predecessors, although some British brewers are now throwing tradition to the wind and using American hops in the name of creativity and marketability. This is fun but certainly blurs the lines of regionality.

PAIRING: *Pale Ale, Sierra Nevada Brewing Co. (USA)*

Sierra Nevada is the iconic American Pale Ale, and is the prototype of what a great APA should be: flavourful and balanced. It was therefore an easy choice for the pairing. The mango pickle with the cod makes the dish very aromatic and fragrant. If you're not familiar with it, mango pickle is an amazing flavour booster for any dish. Its aromas of fenugreek, coriander and mustard seed link beautifully with the beer's notes of pink grapefruit zest and orange flower. Just as the hops are at the forefront of the beer, so too are the aromatics of the pickle.

This pairing is largely based on aromatic compatibility. The two sides combined make for a wonderful bouquet of fragrance. But we still need to consider weight and intensity. I chose a fish substantial enough to not be lost behind the beer or the pickle (salmon, halibut or monkfish would also be great with this recipe). The asparagus and tomatoes can be overlooked as they are tasty but are not the star attractions or main flavour providers. Both sides of the pairing are similar in their weight and have similar intensity of flavour making this pairing a flavourful success.

OTHERS TO TRY:

Pale 31, Firestone Walker Brewing Company (USA)
Canuck Pale Ale, Great Lakes Brewery (Canada)
AFO, Birrificio del Ducato (Italy)

{ AMERICAN PALE ALE }

Roasted Cod *with* Mango Pickle

*You'll find mango pickle at any Indian grocery store; if they don't have it,
lime pickle will work just as well.*

3 Tbsp (45 mL) olive oil

1 lb (500 g) asparagus, tough ends trimmed

2 cups (500 mL) cherry tomatoes

Salt to taste

4 boneless, skinless cod fillets, 5 oz (150 g) each

⅓ cup (80 mL) mango pickle, or more if needed

¼ cup (60 mL) cilantro leaves

Lime halves for garnish

Additional mango pickle to serve

1. Preheat the oven to 450°F (230°C).

2. Drizzle the oil on a rimmed baking sheet. Spread out the asparagus and tomatoes on baking sheet, then shake gently to coat the vegetables with oil. Season with salt to taste.

3. Slide the vegetables to one end of the baking sheet. Lay a piece of foil large enough to hold the cod fillets on the exposed end of baking sheet.

4. Place the cod fillets on the foil, arranging so they are not touching. Pull the foil up around the cod, making more space for the vegetables but not covering the cod completely.

5. Spread the mango pickle over the top of each fillet to cover it completely. Roast just until the cod flakes easily with a fork, 15 to 18 minutes, depending on the thickness of the fillets.

6. Divide the cod fillets, asparagus and tomatoes among four dinner plates. Scatter with cilantro, garnish with lime halves and serve with additional mango pickle if desired.

Serves 4

Czech Pilsner

{ CHICKEN SCHNITZEL *with* APRICOT, GRUYÈRE *and* ARUGULA SALAD }

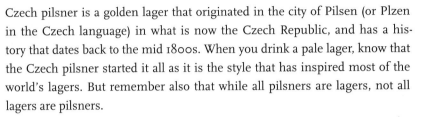

Czech pilsner is a golden lager that originated in the city of Pilsen (or Plzen in the Czech language) in what is now the Czech Republic, and has a history that dates back to the mid 1800s. When you drink a pale lager, know that the Czech pilsner started it all as it is the style that has inspired most of the world's lagers. But remember also that while all pilsners are lagers, not all lagers are pilsners.

Pilsner is a cold-fermented beer with a refreshing, clean character. The type of water used to brew pilsner is low in hard minerals which means it produces a beer with a soft, round mouthfeel compared to its neighbour, the German lager known as pils (page 128). Softness is one of this beer's defining characteristics. The beer is brewed using pilsner malt balanced with the noble Czech variety of hops called Saaz, which lend gentle floral and spice notes to the beer, as well as a noticeable amount of bitterness. Overall, Czech pilsners have a toasted bread aroma, moderate carbonation, a clean, crisp mouthfeel, and a perceivable amount of bitterness from middle to end.

PAIRING: *Pilsner Urquell (Czech Republic)*

Pilsner Urquell is the iconic Czech pilsner (urquell means "the original source" in German) so look for characteristic aromas of earthiness and florality, along with some notes of grass and hay. The malt delivers a straightforward toasted biscuit flavour with a touch of caramel, and it finishes with an astringent herbal bitterness. I chose to team a chicken schnitzel with the beer; for one, it just makes sense—schnitzel and beer, need I say more? But there are technical reasons, too, why this pairing works. The breading on the chicken complements the biscuit flavours of the malt, and the bitterness from the hops helps to clear the palate of any oiliness from the frying. The greens, apricots and fennel bring a welcome freshness and vibrancy to the dish and link well with the hops' floral nature. Overall this classic pairing is pleasant and straightforward.

OTHERS TO TRY:

B:Original, Czechvar (Czech Republic)
Steam Whistle Pilsner (Canada)
Lagunitas Pils (USA)

{ CZECH PILSNER }

Chicken Schnitzel *with* Apricot, Gruyère *and* Arugula Salad

¼ cup (60 mL) all-purpose flour, plus more if needed

2 eggs

3 Tbsp (45 mL) milk

1 cup (250 mL) dried bread crumbs

2 Tbsp (30 mL) coarsely chopped marjoram or oregano

1½ lb (750 g) boneless, skinless chicken breasts, sliced into 1 inch (2.5 cm)-thick cutlets

Salt and freshly ground black pepper to taste

¼ cup (60 mL) olive oil

Additional olive oil for drizzling (optional)

Apricot, Gruyère and Arugula Salad (recipe follows)

1. Spread the flour on a plate. In a small bowl, lightly beat together the eggs and milk until well combined. In a medium bowl, combine the bread crumbs and marjoram.

2. Season the chicken on both sides with salt and pepper. Using a fork to turn chicken, dredge the cutlets in flour to coat on both sides. One at a time, dip each piece of chicken into the egg mixture, then dredge in the bread crumbs to coat well on both sides.

3. In a large skillet or sauté pan, heat the oil over medium-high heat. Working in batches, cook the chicken until golden brown and cooked through, about 4 minutes per side. Set aside and keep warm while you cook the remaining chicken.

4. Divide the chicken schnitzels among four plates and drizzle with additional olive oil (if using). Serve the salad alongside.

Serves 4

Apricot, Gruyère *and* Arugula Salad

1 tsp (5 mL) Dijon mustard

2 tsp (10 mL) white wine vinegar

3 Tbsp (45 mL) olive oil

6 cups (1.4 L) lightly packed washed and dried arugula

5 oz (150 g) Gruyère cheese, cubed

½ cup (125 mL) thinly sliced fennel

3 ripe apricots, pitted and sliced into wedges

Salt and freshly ground black pepper to taste

1. In a large bowl, whisk together the mustard and vinegar to combine. Whisk in the oil.

2. Add the arugula, cheese, fennel and apricots to the bowl. Toss the salad ingredients to combine, then season with salt and pepper to taste.

Serves 4

Doppelbock

{ RACK *of* LAMB *with* PISTACHIO-DIJON CRUST }

Doppelbocks are rich, strong lagers that have a full, sweet maltiness. They come from the Bavarian region of Germany where they were originally brewed by monks who consumed them during their fasting periods. The monks believed the rich, sweet beers had more nutrients than lighter versions and were a healthier alternative when they weren't eating. The beers also have a higher alcohol content—7 to 10% ABV—which perhaps made the act of fasting more bearable.

Expect malty sweetness and warmth from the high alcohol levels, and an aroma that is all about the malt rather than hops. Doppelbocks can range in colour from deep golden to amber-tinged brown. Their full mouthfeel, which gives them the same weight as many meat dishes, means they pair well with heartier fare.

PAIRING: *Höss Doppel-Hirsch,*
Privatbrauerei Höss der Hirschbräu (Germany)

This pairing is all about luxurious gratification. The concept for the pairing is based on the complementary relationship between the flavour and textures of both beer and food. We are not dealing with a lot of contrast for this one as they both offer up succulent, unabashed richness and similar personalities. The sweet richness of the lamb (make sure to not cook it past medium-rare) echoes the sweet maltiness and round, warming alcohol level of the beer which clocks in at 7.2% ABV.

This doppelbock is full of lovely aromas of roasted nuts, brown sugar and dried figs that match superbly with the meat. These notes add so much to each mouthful of food that the beer actually works as a flavourful sauce for the lamb. Additionally, the pistachios, bread crumbs and browned butter in the crust mimic the toasty notes of the beer. When we look for contrast to all this richness we find enough carbonation to do the job. But what this pairing is really asking of you is to sit back and enjoy its lushness and extravagance.

OTHERS TO TRY:

Celebrator Doppelbock, Privatbrauerei Ayinger (Germany)
Salvator Doppelbock, Brauerei Paulaner (Germany)
Captivator Doppelbock, Tree Brewing Co. (Canada)

{ DOPPELBOCK }

Rack *of* Lamb *with* Pistachio-Dijon Crust

½ cup (125 mL) dried bread crumbs

¼ cup (60 mL) finely chopped shelled, unsalted pistachios

1 tsp (5 mL) finely chopped thyme

3 Tbsp (45 mL) unsalted butter

Salt and freshly ground black pepper to taste

2 Tbsp (30 mL) vegetable oil

2 lamb racks, frenched (meat cleaned off the ends of the bones), each about 1½ lb (750 g)

¼ cup (60 mL) Dijon mustard

Thyme sprigs for garnish

1. Preheat the oven to 400°F (200°C).

2. In a medium bowl, stir together the bread crumbs, pistachios and thyme.

3. In a large thick-bottomed skillet, melt the butter over low heat until it is lightly browned, taking care not to burn it. Add the melted butter to the bread crumbs, and stir to combine. Season with salt and pepper to taste.

4. In the same skillet (no need to wash it), heat the vegetable oil over medium-high heat. Season the lamb racks generously with salt and pepper and add to the skillet fat sides down.

5. Cook the lamb racks until golden and their fat is rendered, about 4 minutes. Flip the racks and cook until golden on the other side, about 3 minutes. Remove the skillet from heat, flip the racks fat sides up and let cool slightly.

6. Slather the fat sides of the lamb racks with the mustard. Cover the mustard with the bread-crumb mixture, patting gently so it adheres.

7. Place the lamb racks on a rack set in a roasting pan. Roast until a meat thermometer inserted in the meaty portion of the lamb racks, but not touching any bone, registers 130°F (55°C), 20 to 25 minutes. Let the lamb racks rest for 5 minutes before slicing between the bones, serving two to three ribs per person. Garnish with thyme.

Serves 4

Amber Ale

{ BEEF TENDERLOIN *with* BÉARNAISE AÏOLI }

Amber ale was created by American craft brewers in the 1980s and is a uniquely American style. The term "amber ale" was introduced as a means to distinguish the beers from pale ales, which had a similar colour but were different in flavour and, over time, developed into a formally recognized beer style. There is a fair amount of variation within the style category but expect a malty, well-balanced beer with noticeable hopping. The well-toasted malt offers up notes of toffee and nuts, and has a sweetish, caramel flavour. Amber ale is less bitter than American Pale Ale (see page 68) and is less aromatically bold, but the hops in amber ale are still noticeable and can offer a variety of flavours depending on which hops are used. In short, an amber ale is well balanced and delivers a solid amount of flavour and some malt sweetness, along with a hop aroma, without being too hop-forward.

In a well-made amber ale, the hop bitterness, malt sweetness and aromatic intensity are all harmonious and well aligned. And, since no one component of the beer overshadows another, it's very versatile when it comes to food pairing. Amber ale may not be as flashy as other beer styles but sometimes that's exactly what you want.

PAIRING: *Henderson's Best, Henderson Brewing Co. (Canada)*

For this pairing, I considered the food first, not the beer. Beef tenderloin is a light, lean cut perfect for spring, and tarragon is one of the first herbs to offer up its delicious licoricey leaves once the mild weather arrives. The Béarnaise aïoli, with its herbaceous and zippy personality, adds flavour support to the mild-tasting tenderloin, while its silky texture works wonderfully with the meat.

Then I turned my attention to the beer. This one works because its moderate hopping doesn't overwhelm the aïoli so the intensity of both food and beer are in perfect balance. The malt offers up delicious notes of toffee and treacle tart which are great aromatic complements with the caramelized charring on the exterior of the beef. On the whole, all the aromas and flavours of this pairing work well together but we also need some contrast, and that comes from the herbal bitterness and moderate carbonation, making this pairing a winner on all fronts.

OTHERS TO TRY:

Rogue American Amber Ale (USA)
Yakima Red, Meantime (England)
Ruby Tears, Parallel 49 Brewing Company (Canada)

{ AMBER ALE }

Beef Tenderloin *with* Béarnaise Aïoli

Using a blender to make the Béarnaise is swift and easy and results in a sauce with all the finesse of the classic version.

1½ lb (750 g) beef tenderloin, trimmed

Salt and freshly ground black pepper to taste

2 Tbsp (30 mL) vegetable or olive oil

¼ cup (60 mL) unsalted butter

¼ cup (60 mL) coarsely chopped tarragon stalks

¼ cup (60 mL) plus 1 tsp (5 mL) white wine vinegar, divided

1 large shallot, peeled and finely diced (about 1 Tbsp/15 mL)

2 egg yolks

1 tsp (5 mL) Dijon mustard

2 tsp (10 mL) finely chopped tarragon leaves

Lemon slices and tarragon sprigs for garnish

Freshly cooked frozen or homemade fries to serve (optional)

Dressed green salad to serve (optional)

1. Preheat the oven to 400°F (200°C).

2. Season the beef generously with salt and pepper. In a large ovenproof skillet, heat the oil over medium-high heat. Sear the beef on all sides until it is dark golden, about 5 minutes per side.

3. Transfer the skillet to the oven and roast until a meat thermometer inserted into the thickest part of the beef registers 130°F (55°C) for medium-rare, about 15 minutes.

4. While the beef is cooking, in a small saucepan over low heat (or in the microwave), warm the butter just until melted, then set aside.

5. In a second small saucepan, combine the tarragon stalks, ¼ cup (60 mL) white wine vinegar and shallot. Simmer over medium-low heat until the vinegar is reduced to 1 tablespoonful. Strain the vinegar into a blender, discarding solids.

6. Add the remaining vinegar, egg yolks, mustard and ½ tsp (2 mL) salt to the blender. Pulse until smooth. With the machine running on low speed, slowly drizzle in the melted butter. Pour slowly until the mixture begins to thicken, then continue to slowly drizzle in the butter until it is all incorporated. Scrape the sauce into a small bowl, stir in the chopped tarragon leaves and season with pepper to taste. Set aside until ready to serve. (If not serving right away, cover and refrigerate for up to 3 days.)

7. When the beef is ready, let it rest for 5 minutes before slicing. Garnish with lemon slices and tarragon and serve with the Béarnaise aïoli, and French fries, if desired. A green salad is the perfect addition to round out this meal.

Serves 4

SUMMER

PALE LAGER 86
Salt Cod Fritters with Spicy Mango Chutney Dip 88

GOSE 90
Seared Calamari with Green Olives, Tomato and Lemon 92

FRUIT LAMBIC 94
Rustic Terrine with Cherries and Pistachios 96

MUNICH HELLES 98
Steamed Clams with Chorizo and Tomatoes 100

GLUTEN-FREE BEER 102
Seared Halloumi with Lentils, Peaches and Pomegranate 104

FRUIT BEER 106
Salmon with Nectarine, Raspberry and Avocado Salad 108

INDIA PALE ALE 110
Roast Chicken Tacos with Pineapple Salsa 112

RAUCHBIER 114
Grilled Burgers with Bacon-Onion Relish and Smoky Aïoli 116

HEFEWEIZEN 118
Flank Steak with Corn Relish and Cheddar Grits 120

DRY STOUT 122
French Roast Ribs 124

Pale Lager

{ SALT COD FRITTERS *with* SPICY MANGO CHUTNEY DIP }

If you grew up in North America during the 1980s or earlier, the first beer you likely ever tried was a pale lager. Maybe this is the beer your dad rewarded himself with after having cut the lawn on a hot, sunny day. It is a style that is enjoyed the world over. Regarding colour, taste and quality, there is a broad spectrum to pale lagers, but all have in common a great ability to quench thirst. Pale lager is fairly light in colour, moderately carbonated, typically with subtle, balanced malt and hop aromas. The alcohol level can range from 4 to 5.5% ABV which makes them quite sessionable (as in easy drinking, low-alcohol beers), especially when served nicely chilled.

PAIRING: *Moosehead Lager (Canada)*

These salt cod fritters pair well with a pale lager due to the beer's refreshing quaffable nature. The fritters are addictive and, as you reach for your third and fourth, you'll want a beer to wash down every delicious bite. This lager's 5% alcohol level allows for you to do this without incident.

A beer with moderate carbonation is perfect with salty, fried food like this, as it cleanses the palate of any oiliness from the fritters or richness from the mango chutney dip, plus the beer's sweet, malty nature tempers the heat of the hot pepper sauce and black pepper. In addition, the lager's moderate hop bitterness is a great contrast to the salty bits of fried cod.

Although the cod is battered and deep-fried, the baking powder lightens any potential heaviness in the batter, which means the fritters and beer are on par in regard to weight. One of the signs of a great pairing is when your bite of food stimulates your desire for another sip, and vice versa. You could call it a vicious circle if it wasn't so delightful.

OTHERS TO TRY:

Craft Lager, Muskoka Brewery (Canada)
Birra Moretti (Italy)
Stella Artois Premium Lager (Belgium)

{ PALE LAGER }

Salt Cod Fritters *with* Spicy Mango Chutney Dip

8 oz (250 g) skinless, boneless salt cod, cut into 2-inch (5 cm) chunks

½ cup (125 mL) mango chutney

2 tsp (10 mL) lime juice

½ cup (125 mL) mayonnaise

Your favourite hot sauce to taste, such as Sriracha, Tabasco or Jamaican hot sauce

1 plum tomato, coarsely chopped

2 green onions, coarsely chopped

¼ cup (60 mL) coarsely chopped cilantro

1 cup (250 mL) all-purpose flour

1 tsp (5 mL) baking powder

Pinch of ground cloves (optional)

Freshly ground black pepper to taste

6 cups (1.4 L) vegetable oil

Salt to taste

Lime wedges to serve

1. Place the cod in a medium bowl and add enough cold water to cover it. Refrigerate for 24 hours, changing the water at least once.

2. For the mango chutney dip, stir together the mango chutney and lime juice in a small bowl until well combined. Stir in the mayonnaise and hot sauce to taste. Refrigerate until ready to serve.

3. Drain the cod and pulse it in a food processor until chopped into pea-sized pieces. Add the tomato, green onions and cilantro and continue to pulse until the ingredients are coarsely chopped and evenly distributed throughout the cod.

4. Scrape the mixture out into a medium bowl. Stir in the flour, baking powder, cloves (if using) and a generous grinding of pepper. Gradually stir in ½ cup (125 mL) water until a thick pancake-like batter forms, adding a splash more water if the mixture is too thick.

5. In a medium pot, heat the oil over medium-high heat. Add a tiny dollop of batter to the oil; if the batter bubbles and rises, the oil is hot enough.

6. Using a tablespoonful of batter per fritter and working in batches, fry the fritters by carefully sliding the batter into the oil. As each batch is cooked, remove the fritters from the oil with a slotted spoon, place on a plate lined with paper towel and season with salt.

7. When all the fritters are cooked, serve them with lime wedges and the mango chutney dip.

Serves 4 as a snack

Gose

{ SEARED CALAMARI *with* GREEN OLIVES, TOMATO *and* LEMON }

Gose, an unfiltered, effervescent wheat beer brewed with the addition of varying amounts of coriander seeds and salt, is a distinctive beer style from Germany. First made in the 16th century, it is a historic style that is gaining traction as innovative brewers look to lesser-known types of beer to create new and unique products. Traditionally, there is no fruit added to Gose but modern interpretations of the style sometimes include citrus or stone fruit, cucumber or melon to add another element of interest to the beer.

Gose is considered part of the sour beer family which also includes Berliner Weisse, Gueuze (page 60) and Flanders Red (page 140) among others. Traditionally the sourness in Gose comes from the naturally occurring bacteria called lactobacillus, which creates an appealing acidic characteristic when kept in check. Nowadays, breweries are free of such bacteria, so the beers are inoculated intentionally.

There is no apparent aroma nor bitterness from the hops, and the malt delivers a breadiness on the nose but no sweetness on the palate. This is a very dry beer with all its components making for a very intriguing food-friendly summertime drink.

PAIRING: *Original Ritterguts Gose (Germany)*

I chose to pair this calamari dish with the Gose because the food and beer share so many similarities and are great complements for each other. The beer offers up tart lemon notes reminiscent of a homemade lemon curd, and has refreshing aromas of pink grapefruit zest and fresh ginger. The citric tartness replays in the flavour and works like a spritz of lemon over the calamari. There is an elegance in the balance of this beer—it is tart with just enough malt character to keep it balanced, and a fine effervescence to gently cut through the olive oil-based sauce. The beer's tartness enlivens and helps amplify the flavours in the calamari, and its subtle salinity perfectly complements the brininess of the olives. If I had to pick a favourite pairing in the book, this one would be the winner.

OTHERS TO TRY:

Prophets & Nomads Gose, Collective Arts Brewing (Canada)
Briney Melon Gose, Anderson Valley Brewing Company (USA)
Leipzig Gose, Bayerischer Bahnhof (Germany)

{ GOSE }

Seared Calamari *with* **Green Olives, Tomato** *and* **Lemon**

2 lb (1 kg) whole calamari, cleaned, beaks removed and tentacles separated from bodies (about 12 squid)

¼ cup (60 mL) olive oil, divided

2 tsp (10 mL) finely chopped garlic

¼ tsp (1 mL) chili flakes

2 cups (500 mL) cherry tomatoes, halved lengthwise

½ cup (125 mL) large pimento-stuffed green olives, halved

Finely grated zest and squeezed juice of 1 lemon

2 Tbsp (30 mL) coarsely chopped basil

1. Using a small, sharp knife, cut a lengthwise slit in each calamari body and open like a book; they should lie flat. With the knife, score a crosshatch pattern in the outer side of the flesh, making six cuts in both directions and trying to avoid slicing right through (although it's not a big problem if you do). This will allow the calamari to soak up more flavour. Pat the calamari bodies and tentacles dry with paper towel.

2. In a large skillet, heat 2 Tbsp (30 mL) olive oil over medium-high heat. Lay the bodies flat in the skillet and cook until browned and starting to curl up, about 2 minutes. Flip the bodies over. Add the tentacles to the skillet. Stir well and let everything cook through, about 3 more minutes. Remove the calamari from the skillet and set aside.

3. Reduce the heat to medium and add 1 Tbsp (15 mL) of the remaining olive oil to the skillet, along with the garlic and chili flakes. Cook, stirring, for 1 minute.

4. Add the tomatoes, olives, and lemon zest and juice. Cook, stirring occasionally, until the tomatoes are tender, about 4 minutes.

5. Return the calamari to the skillet and warm it through in the tomato mixture for 1 minute. Add the basil and remaining olive oil, and stir to combine. Divide among four plates and serve.

Serves 4

Fruit Lambic

{ RUSTIC TERRINE *with* CHERRIES *and* PISTACHIOS }

Don't confuse fruit lambic with fruit beer (for more on fruit beer, see page 106). Fruit lambic is made with a base of lambic beer, the sour Belgian beer fermented by the wild yeasts and bacteria in the area surrounding Brussels. Unlike fruit beer, fruit lambic is flavoured with fruit after fermentation not before. The fruit—most commonly cherries or raspberries—is added to the aging barrels and over time the yeast and bacteria "eat" and ferment the fruit.

Despite the addition of fruit, a classic fruit lambic is a very dry beer. Sweet versions do exist but these are an attempt to appeal to a larger audience, and are more about marketing than tradition.

A fruit lambic will have aromas of whatever fruit was added; for example kriek will have notes of cherry, and framboise those of raspberry. However, these fruit flavours won't be shiny and bright. Remember, the fruit was slowly devoured by bacteria and will contribute a more rustic personality than would the fresh versions of the fruit. The beer will also have the wild, barnyardy aromas and tart, refreshing taste of a regular lambic.

PAIRING: *Cuvée des Jacobins Kriek (Belgium)*

In addition to pairing successfully in terms of flavour, taste and texture, this match also works on a psychological level, or more simply put: feeling. Just the thought of eating a peasant-style terrine while drinking an earthy, rustic beer from the lush countryside of Flanders makes so much sense, even if you don't know what either of them taste like. Am I right? This terrine and fruit lambic combination is a perfect example of a psychological pairing that works. It gives satisfaction even before you've taken a sniff, sip or bite.

The herbs and dried spices in the terrine are a great nod to the subtle herbaceousness and spicy, rosewood aroma of the beer, while the cherries that dot the terrine link to the beer's delicate flavour of old-fashioned cherry lozenges. In the mouth, the kriek offers all the lemony acidity needed to balance the salty richness delivered from the pork and prosciutto, which keeps the pairing bright and fresh. The last component that makes this pairing come together brilliantly is the rusticity of beer and terrine. Both have a similar personality of sophisticated simplicity, giving a sense of times past when you ate the food that your fields provided.

OTHERS TO TRY:

Framboise, Brouwerij Lindemans (Belgium)
Oud Kriek, Brouwerij 3 Fonteinen (Belgium)
Rosé de Gambrinus, Cantillon (Belgium)

{ FRUIT LAMBIC }

Rustic Terrine *with* Cherries *and* Pistachios

This hearty terrine is even better the next day, after the flavours have had a chance to develop. Simply wrap it tightly and refrigerate overnight. Before serving, let the refrigerated terrine stand at room temperature for 30 minutes or so before serving.

3 Tbsp (45 mL) unsalted butter

1 cup (250 mL) finely chopped shallots

2 Tbsp (30 mL) finely chopped thyme

2 Tbsp (30 mL) finely chopped garlic

1½ tsp (7 mL) ground nutmeg

1 tsp (5 mL) ground allspice

½ tsp (2 mL) ground cardamom

12 thin slices prosciutto

4 slices bacon, cut into 1 inch (2.5 cm) pieces

½ lb (250 g) ground pork

1 lb (500 g) chicken livers, rinsed and drained

1 egg

¼ cup (60 mL) whipping cream (35%)

2 tsp (10 mL) salt

1 tsp (5 mL) lemon juice

1 cup (250 mL) pitted, halved ripe cherries

½ cup (125 mL) shelled unsalted pistachios

Cornichons, grainy mustard and good bread to serve

1. Preheat the oven to 325°F (160°C).

2. In a small saucepan, melt the butter over medium heat. Add the shallots, thyme and garlic, and cook, stirring occasionally, until the shallots are translucent, about 12 minutes. Stir in the nutmeg, allspice and cardamom. Set aside to cool slightly.

3. Line a 9-by-5-inch (23-by-13-cm) loaf pan or 5-cup (1.2 L) terrine dish with the prosciutto by overlapping the slices and allowing them to overhang the edge of the pan. The slices will eventually wrap over the top of meat mixture once it is placed in the pan.

4. Pulse the bacon in a food processor until coarsely chopped. Add the ground pork and pulse again to break up the meat.

5. Add the shallot mixture, chicken livers, egg, cream, salt and lemon juice. Pulse a few times to coarsely chop the livers.

6. Remove the blade from the food processor and gently stir the cherries and pistachios into the meat mixture.

7. Scrape the meat mixture into the prepared pan and smooth the surface level. Fold the overhanging prosciutto over the meat mixture. Cover the loaf pan tightly with foil and place it in a larger roasting pan. Pour enough hot water into the roasting pan to come halfway up the side of the loaf pan.

8. Bake for 1 hour and 45 minutes. Remove the foil and continue to bake until a meat thermometer inserted in the terrine registers 160°F (70°C) and the top of the terrine is lightly browned, about 15 minutes more.

9. Pour off the excess liquid from the loaf pan. Carefully unmold the terrine onto a serving platter and let cool to room temperature. Serve cut into slices, with cornichons, mustard and bread.

Serves 8 as appetizer or 4 as light lunch

Munich Helles

{ STEAMED CLAMS *with* CHORIZO *and* TOMATOES }

Helles is a German beer style, and one of the country's most popular due to its easy drinking nature. The word "helles" means "light" and refers to the brightness of the beer. It is a pale lager which leans more toward malt aroma than hop. It has a sweet malty, bread-like nose and can have subtle notes of florality and spiciness. Although the beer has a rounded, sweet malt mouthfeel, it is balanced nicely with a judicious use of traditional German hops. Its roundness is what makes it such a versatile beer for pairing with food, and a pleasant bready backdrop for whatever you eat with it.

PAIRING: *Hofbräu Original (Germany)*

Let's think. What is the ideal accompaniment to juicy, soppy clams and sauce? Bread, of course. And that is why a helles is the perfect pairing for steamed clams: it is bread captured in liquid form. Here, we're looking at complementary, not contrasting, flavours. The biscuity, bready notes of this straightforward lager are just what the dish needs. Between the flavourful chorizo, mineral-like clams and rich tomato sauce, we don't need an overly complex beer. The subtle straw and floral aromas are pleasing accents, yet they don't get in the way. And the sweet, round mouthfeel prevents the spice of the chorizo from taking over, something a thinner beer would not be able to do.

OTHERS TO TRY:

Weihenstephaner Original (Germany)
Hacker-Pschorr Munich Gold (Germany)
Spaten Munich Helles (Germany)

{ MUNICH HELLES }

Steamed Clams *with* Chorizo *and* Tomatoes

2 Tbsp (30 mL) olive oil

1 lb (500 g) raw chorizo or hot Italian sausage, removed from casings and broken into grape-sized pieces

¾ cup (175 mL) finely chopped onions

½ tsp (2 mL) sweet smoked paprika

1 cup (250 mL) finely diced plum tomatoes

½ cup (125 mL) beer (preferably what you're serving with the clams, or a flavourful German-style lager)

2 lb (1 kg) littleneck clams

2 Tbsp (30 mL) finely chopped parsley

Toasted bread to serve

1. In a large pot, heat the oil over medium-high. Add the sausage and cook, stirring often, until browned, about 10 minutes.

2. Add the onions to the pot and cook, stirring often, until transparent, about 8 minutes. Stir in the paprika, then add the tomatoes and beer. Cook, stirring often, for 5 minutes.

3. Add the clams and cover the pot. Reduce the heat to medium and cook, stirring occasionally, until the clams open fully, 10 to 15 minutes. Discard any clams that do not open.

4. Divide among four shallow bowls and sprinkle with parsley. Serve with toasted bread.

Serves 4

Gluten-Free Beer

{ SEARED HALLOUMI *with* LENTILS, PEACHES *and* POMEGRANATE }

Gluten-free beer is not a beer style, but a category that is becoming more popular as consumers seek alternatives to barley and wheat. Once upon a time, gluten-free beer didn't taste so good and there were few options available. Nowadays, there are gluten-free beers in all sorts of styles, from lagers to IPAs to Saisons. Some are brewed using alternative grains, such as rice, sorghum, millet, spelt or buckwheat; others are made with barley that has been processed to remove or reduce its gluten content.

PAIRING: *Daura, Damm Brewery (Spain)*

Simply put, the chief reason this pairing works is there is gluten in neither the food nor the beer. But we want more out of the pairing than just that. Here I wanted to show that gluten-free can be delicious and full of flavour. The beer's style is that of a pale lager, and it delivers a honeyed nose of fresh bread crusts and sweet malt, both of which complement the peaches and pomegranate in the salad. I've added the cutting bitterness of arugula to keep things interesting, and the earthy nature of the lentils echoes that of the hops. Another successful element is the cleansing effect of the beer's carbonation on the rich, salty, rubbery nature of the halloumi. All in all, for a vegetarian dish teamed with a gluten-free beer, this pairing achieves the goal of being complex and interesting. Enjoy!

OTHERS TO TRY:

Pale Ale, Omission Brewing Co. (USA)
Bohemian Pilsner, Bellfield Brewery (Scotland)
Forager Lager, Whistler Brewing Co. (Canada)

{ GLUTEN-FREE BEER }

Seared Halloumi *with* Lentils, Peaches *and* Pomegranate

6 oz (175 g) halloumi cheese

¼ cup (60 mL) olive oil, divided

1 cup (250 mL) cooked green lentils (or drained and rinsed, if canned)

4 cups (960 mL) lightly packed washed and dried arugula

2 ripe peaches, pitted and sliced into wedges

½ cup (125 mL) pomegranate seeds

¼ cup (60 mL) coarsely torn mint leaves

2 Tbsp (30 mL) white or red wine vinegar

1. Slice the halloumi into 8 even-sized slices and set aside to soak in a bowl of cold water for up to 20 minutes. When ready to cook, drain the halloumi and pat dry with paper towel.

2. In a large skillet, heat 2 Tbsp (30 mL) of the oil over medium-high heat. Fry the halloumi until golden, about 1 minute. Flip the cheese over and cook until golden on the other side, 1 minute more. Remove the halloumi from the skillet and set aside.

3. Divide the lentils among four bowls. Top with the arugula, peaches, pomegranate seeds and mint, dividing evenly.

4. Stir together the remaining olive oil and vinegar and drizzle evenly over each salad. Top each salad with 2 pieces of halloumi and serve.

Serves 4

Fruit Beer

{ SALMON *with* NECTARINE, RASPBERRY *and* AVOCADO SALAD }

Fruit beer is a broad category that has one thing in common: fruit. But, the style can be made from a dizzying array of fruit ranging from berries, such as raspberries, cherries or strawberries, to more exotic interpretations using papaya, mango or pineapple. The options are near endless. Whatever fruit the brewer chooses, it might be added fresh, raw or as sweetened, artificially flavoured syrup, and all of these affect the quality and sweetness level of the beer.

Fruit beers can be created using different "base" beer styles. Some fruit beers are brewed as wheat beers, some are built on the foundation of a pale ale; even stout can be brewed with fruit and considered a fruit beer. So, when drinking a fruit beer, expect to taste not only the flavour of the fruit that has been added, but also the typical characteristics of the base beer.

PAIRING: *Éphémère Sureau, Unibroue (Canada)*

This elegant fruit wheat beer from Québec is made using both the elderberry and its blossoms, which ends up producing a wonderfully aromatic beer filled with white floral and red berry notes, and an exotic muskmelon aroma. This pairing works well not least because of aesthetics—the salmon and beer are undeniably beautiful together. This is a great start given that we eat with our eyes first, but the pairing also works on a technical level. The beer's floral and cranberry notes are good aromatic complements to the raspberries and nectarines in the salad. Along with the beer's pretty fruit-related aromas, there are the typical zesty lemony wheat notes and a clean, biscuity melba toast flavour that pair nicely with the elements on the plate.

Another reason the pairing works so well is the beer's palate-cleansing acidity. Its pleasant tartness is the perfect tool for cutting through the richness of the salmon and avocado. The elusive goal when pairing food and beer is to achieve a result that is greater than the sum of its parts. With each mouthful here a bright, balanced and flavourful combination, this one's a real winner.

OTHERS TO TRY:

Sea Rose Tart Cherry Wheat Ale, Ballast Point (USA)
Apricot Wheat Ale, St-Ambroise (Canada)
La Choulette Framboise (France)

{ FRUIT BEER }

Salmon *with* Nectarine, Raspberry *and* Avocado Salad

¼ cup (60 mL) olive oil, divided

1 Tbsp (15 mL) raspberry vinegar (white or red wine vinegar will also do)

1½ tsp (7 mL) Dijon mustard

6 cups (1.4 L) lightly packed washed and dried frisée lettuce, torn into bite-sized pieces

2 ripe nectarines, pitted and each sliced into six wedges

1 ripe avocado, pitted, peeled and sliced

Salt to taste

4 boneless salmon fillets with skin (each about 6 oz/175 g)

Pepper to taste

½ cup (125 mL) raspberries

1. In a large bowl and using a fork, whisk together 3 Tbsp (45 mL) oil, the vinegar and mustard. Add the lettuce, nectarines and avocado. Season with salt to taste and toss gently to combine. Set aside.

2. In a large nonstick skillet, heat the remaining oil over medium-high heat. Season the salmon with salt and pepper to taste and place, skin-side down, in the skillet. Allow the skin to crisp before flipping the salmon, about 5 minutes. Cook the salmon on the second side until just cooked through, about 4 more minutes.

3. Add the raspberries to the salad. Toss the salad again, then divide among four plates. Place the salmon alongside the salad, and serve.

Serves 4

India Pale Ale

{ ROAST CHICKEN TACOS *with* PINEAPPLE SALSA }

India Pale Ale (IPA) is a beer that has taken the beer world by storm; almost every North American brewery brews one. For all it is trendy, it is a beer style with a history behind it, and was actually created in 18th-century England more out of necessity than anything else. At the time, beers shipped to the British-ruled colony of India were arriving spoiled and undrinkable after the long, tumultuous journey across the sea. To better survive the journey, breweries began making higher-alcohol beers and giving them a good dose of dry-hopping. The alcohol fortified the beer and the hops preserved it, allowing the beers to be "strong" enough to arrive intact. This more robust and flavourful beer became so popular, it was not only brewed for export, but also for the British domestic market.

Jump forward a couple of centuries—give or take a few years—and the hoppy IPA style has found solid footing in North America. These days when people talk about IPAs they are usually referring to an American-style IPA that is heavily hopped, has an ABV of 6 to 7% and an explosive nose of juicy, bright hop aroma. An American IPA will be brewed with American hops which give the beer the delicious citrus and pine notes that IPA lovers are drawn to.

A classic British-style IPA will be somewhat more modest in its use of hops and brewed with British hop varieties, such as Golding or Fuggle (I never get tired of saying "Fuggle"). But, the bold citrusy American style is so popular worldwide that even British brewers are now using American hop varieties in order to capture some of that hop-hungry market.

PAIRING: *Lagunitas IPA, Lagunitas Brewing Company (USA)*

Nothing says summer quite like a bright, citrusy IPA, and this beer delivers a glass of sunshine. It has vibrant notes of pine and white grapefruit pith on the nose, which carry onto the palate. There is also a subtle, yummy note of caramelized pineapple, making a great aromatic link to the pineapple salsa. The beer's mouthfeel is juicy and round, and delivers scrumptious flavours of toffee and dark toasted bread, which are nice partners to the wonderfully spiced crispy bits of chicken skin and meat. When picking the pairing, I

wanted a dish that would have enough richness to contrast the astringency of the hops, and a big bite of roast chicken, avocado and sour cream are up to the task, while the hop bitterness of the IPA makes easy work of cutting through all that silky richness. The food also needed to be bold enough aromatically to match the flashy personality of an IPA. Tacos, though somewhat cliché, are really a perfect pairing. Crammed full of bright aromas of cilantro, lime, onion, jalapeños and pineapple, they scream summertime!

OTHERS TO TRY:

London IPA, Meantime (England)
Stone IPA (USA)
Ransack the Universe, Collective Arts Brewing (Canada)

{ INDIA PALE ALE }

Roast Chicken Tacos *with* Pineapple Salsa

2 tsp (10 mL) chili powder

2 tsp (10 mL) paprika

2 tsp (10 mL) ground cumin

¾ tsp (4 mL) salt

3 skin-on, bone-in chicken breasts (about 2½ lb/1.25 kg total weight)

2 Tbsp (30 mL) olive oil

12 small flour tortillas

2 ripe avocados, pitted, peeled and sliced

1 cup (250 mL) sour cream

Pineapple Salsa (recipe follows)

Sour cream and your favourite hot sauce to serve

1. Adjust the oven rack to the middle position and preheat the oven to 375°F (190°C).

2. In a small bowl, stir together the chili powder, paprika, cumin and salt. Sprinkle all the spice mixture evenly over both sides of the chicken breasts.

3. In a large skillet, heat the oil over medium-high heat. Place the chicken, skin-side down, in the skillet and cook for 3 minutes. Take care not to burn the spices; reduce the heat if necessary. Flip the chicken and cook on the other side for 3 minutes, again taking care not to burn the spices.

4. Remove from the heat and let the skillet cool slightly, then add ¾ cup (175 mL) water.

5. Transfer the skillet to the oven and cook the chicken until a meat thermometer inserted in the thickest part of the breasts and not touching any bone registers 165°F (75°C), about 25 minutes. If the skillet starts to look dry, add more water, ¼ cup (60 mL) at a time, to prevent scorching.

6. Meanwhile, stack the tortillas and wrap the stack in foil.

7. When the chicken is cooked, remove the skillet from the oven and turn off the oven. Put the stack of tortillas in the oven to warm. Set the chicken aside until it is cool enough to handle.

8. Remove the chicken skin and set aside. Shred the meat, discarding the bones but reserving any cooking juices. Place meat in a bowl and set aside.

9. Coarsely chop the chicken skin (you can use all of it or the skin from just one breast) and place in the bowl with chicken meat and any remaining cooking juices. Stir to combine. Serve the chicken with the warm tortillas, avocados, sour cream, pineapple salsa and your favourite hot sauce.

Serves 4

Pineapple Salsa

½ cup (125 mL) very finely diced red onion

2 Tbsp (30 mL) lime juice

1 Tbsp (15 mL) honey

½ tsp (2 mL) ground cumin

½ tsp (2 mL) salt

2 cups (500 mL) peeled and diced pineapple

1 cup (250 mL) finely diced plum tomatoes

⅓ cup (80 mL) coarsely chopped cilantro

3 Tbsp (45 mL) seeded and thinly sliced jalapeño (or to taste)

In a medium bowl stir together the red onion, lime juice, honey, cumin and salt. Stir in the pineapple, tomatoes, cilantro and jalapeño.

Makes about 3½ cups (850 mL)

Rauchbier

{ GRILLED BURGERS *with* BACON-ONION RELISH *and* SMOKY AÏOLI }

Rauchbier is a unique beer originating in the German city of Bamberg. Brewed using specialty malt that has been smoked with beech wood, it is a lager with a spicy, smoky aroma. While the intensity of the smoke varies from brewer to brewer, Bamberg-style rauchbiers are Märzen-style beers, meaning they are malt-forward amber lagers, so there should also be some sweetish malt aroma coming through alongside the smokiness.

Rauchbiers have a medium mouthfeel and a clean, dry finish and are well suited to charred or heavily roasted foods—think barbecue—so the smokiness makes sense with the food. These beers are great with meats that have inherent fattiness, such as pork shoulder or ribeye, or hard, aged cheeses like Beemster and good-quality cheddar. Rauchbiers have a moderate amount of hopping, enough to give the beers balanced mouthfeel and a little bitterness on the palate but little in the way of hop aroma.

Some creative brewers make different styles, from wheat beers to porters, but these beers are not considered traditional rauchbiers.

PAIRING: *Aecht Schlenkerla Märzen, Brauerei Heller (Germany)*

Summer makes me think of burgers on the grill, so I designed a particularly smoky one to be a great partner to this rauchbier. The beer has a big personality, with smoke its dominant flavour. The burger's first layer of smokiness comes from the addition of smoked paprika, then the grilling process, which creates caramelized charred bits on the patty, amps up the smoke factor even further. Still not enough smoke for you? I topped the burger with onions slowly cooked with smoky bacon, then added a rich, smoky aïoli. These burger fixings not only add flavour but also some sweet unctuousness to make the burger even more juicy. And, speaking of juicy, make sure your beef is not too lean or you will end up with dense, dry burgers. Finally, all this juicy succulence needs a counterbalance, and the beer's carbonation and hop bitterness are more than capable of cutting through the rich sauciness of the burger, refreshing the palate and calling you back for another bite.

OTHERS TO TRY:

Bamberg Castle, Cameron's Brewing (Canada)
Samuel Adams Smoked Lager (USA)
Spezial Rauchbier, Brauerei Spezial (Germany)

{ RAUCHBIER }

Grilled Burgers *with* Bacon-Onion Relish *and* Smoky Aïoli

1½ lb (750 g) ground beef

½ cup (125 mL) grated cheese, such as Beemster, aged cheddar or Gruyère

1 tsp (5 mL) Worcestershire sauce

½ tsp (2 mL) salt

¼ tsp (1 mL) freshly ground black pepper

4 burger buns, split and toasted

Bacon-Onion Relish (recipe follows)

Smoky Aïoli (recipe follows)

1. In a large bowl, mix together the beef, cheese, Worcestershire sauce, salt and pepper. Form the mixture into 4 even-sized patties.

2. Preheat the grill to medium-high and oil the racks. Grill the burgers until lightly charred and cooked through, about 8 minutes per side.

3. Serve the burgers in the buns, along with the bacon-onion relish and smoky aïoli.

——————————————————— *Serves 4*

Bacon-Onion Relish ————————————

1 Tbsp (15 mL) unsalted butter

4 slices bacon, cut into 1 inch (2.5 cm) pieces

1 large Spanish onion, very thinly sliced

¼ tsp (1 mL) salt

½ tsp (2 mL) red or white wine vinegar

1. In a medium saucepan, melt the butter over medium heat. Add the bacon and cook, stirring often, until the bacon is nicely browned and its fat is rendered, about 10 minutes.

2. Add the onion, salt and ¼ cup (60 mL) water. Cover and cook over low heat for 20 minutes, making sure to stir occasionally to prevent burning.

3. Remove the lid and continue to simmer over low heat until all the liquid has reduced and the onions are golden and tender, about 10 minutes. Let cool completely, then stir in the vinegar.

——————————————————— *Makes 1 cup (250 mL)*

Smoky Aïoli ————————————

½ cup (125 mL) mayonnaise

2 tsp (10 mL) smoked paprika

2 tsp (10 mL) your favourite hot sauce (or to taste)

1 tsp (5 mL) Worcestershire sauce

In a small bowl, stir together all the ingredients until well combined.

——————————————————— *Makes about ½ cup (125 mL)*

Hefeweizen

{ FLANK STEAK *with* CORN RELISH *and* CHEDDAR GRITS }

German hefeweizens are cheerful, refreshing ales historically linked to the region of Bavaria in the southeast of the country. It is the German version of wheat beer and is also known as weissbier (white beer) or weizenbier (wheat beer). Hefeweizen (pronounced hay-fuh-vites-zen) is almost as fun to say as it is to drink. The name translates as "yeast wheat," and refers to the suspended, unfiltered yeast that remains in the beer. If the yeast is filtered out of a hefeweizen and the beer is clear, then it is considered a kristallweizen. So many names, so much great beer.

There are a number of elements that make hefeweizen distinct and delicious. It is brewed with at least 50% wheat, which contains more protein than barley and renders the beer hazy and gives it a characteristic mousse-like, long-lasting, over-the-top crown of foam. The wheat and suspended yeast also create a smooth, creamy mouthfeel that is amplified by the beer's highly effervescent nature. One of the telltale traits of German hefeweizen is its aroma; the unique top-fermenting yeast strain used in brewing Bavarian wheat beers produces very perceptible aromas of clove, banana and, sometimes, bubblegum. The beer also has the typical twang of citrus from the wheat. The bright and spritzy personality of hefeweizen, along with its low alcohol of 4.5 to 5.5% ABV, make it a natural companion for food.

PAIRING: *Ayinger Bräu Weisse, Brauerei Ayinger (Germany)*

When choosing a beer pairing for the flank steak, I needed to consider the charred sweetness of the meat, the fresh herbaceousness and zip of the salsa, and the creamy, rich cheese grits. The lively carbonation of this delightful hefeweizen is a great contrast to the beef and grits, its powerful effervescence easily cutting through any fat and heaviness. And the yeasty, bready nature of the beer is a good backdrop to all the different flavours in the dish. This very aromatic relish, with its red onion, lime and cilantro, is complemented perfectly by the hefeweizen's big bold notes of banana custard, spicy clove and

zippy gingersnaps. The creamy texture of the beer gives it great mouthfeel and enough substance to stand up to all that is happening on the plate. Lastly, while hefeweizen goes down well any time of the year, it truly shines during the sunny days of summer.

OTHERS TO TRY:

Big Boot Hefeweizen, Big Rig Brewery (Canada)
Hefe Weissbier, Weinhenstephaner (Germany)
Hula Hefeweizen, Kona Brewing Co. (USA)

{ HEFEWEIZEN }

Flank Steak *with* Corn Relish *and* Cheddar Grits

3 Tbsp (45 mL) olive oil

3 Tbsp (45 mL) lime juice

2 Tbsp (30 mL) packed brown sugar

2 tsp (10 mL) sweet Hungarian paprika

2 tsp (10 mL) chili powder

2 tsp (10 mL) ground cumin

2 tsp (10 mL) finely chopped garlic

¼ tsp (1 mL) ground allspice (optional)

1½ lb (750 g) flank steak, pierced all over on both sides with a fork

Salt to taste

Corn Relish (recipe follows)

Cheddar Grits (recipe follows)

1. In a large bowl or freezer bag, mix together the oil, lime juice, sugar, paprika, chili powder, cumin, garlic and allspice until well combined. Add the flank steak and coat well on both sides with the marinade. Cover if using a bowl, seal if using a bag. Refrigerate for at least 2 hours or until the next day.

2. Preheat the grill to high and oil the racks.

3. Remove the flank steak from the marinade and season generously on both sides with salt. Grill, with the lid partially closed, about 7 minutes per side for medium-rare. Avoid flare-ups and try to get as much char on the steak as possible (without burning it) to develop lots of flavour.

4. Remove the steak from the grill and let it rest for 5 minutes before slicing. Serve with the corn relish and cheddar grits, drizzling with any cooking juices that have accumulated under the steak.

Serves 4

Corn Relish

3 cobs of corn, husked and halved

2 Tbsp (30 mL) olive oil

1 Tbsp (15 mL) lime juice

1 tsp (5 mL) honey

½ tsp (2 mL) salt

2 cups (500 mL) cherry tomatoes, halved lengthwise

¼ cup (60 mL) finely diced red onion

¼ cup (60 mL) coarsely chopped cilantro

Your favourite hot sauce to taste

This relish is extra tasty made with fresh corn but, out of season, you can substitute 2¼ cups (560 mL) rinsed and drained frozen corn kernels. Don't cook but simply add them to the relish along with the hot sauce.

1. Bring a large pot of salted water to a boil over high heat. Add the halved corn cobs and boil for 4 minutes. Drain and rinse under cold running water. Set aside to cool.

2. In a medium bowl, whisk together the oil, lime juice, honey and salt. Add the tomatoes, onion and cilantro and toss well.

3. Using a sharp knife and standing the corn cob halves on their flat ends, slice the kernels from each. Add the kernels to the bowl, along with hot sauce to taste, and toss well.

Makes about 5 cups (1.2 L)

Cheddar Grits

4 cups (960 mL) vegetable or chicken stock

1 cup (250 mL) white corn grits (these are the same as polenta but made with white corn instead of yellow)

1 cup (250 mL) grated cheddar cheese

Salt to taste

1. In a large pot, bring the stock and 2 cups (500 mL) of water to a boil over high heat. Reduce the heat so the stock is simmering. Slowly whisk in the grits. Cover and cook over low heat, stirring occasionally to prevent the grits from splattering and scorching, until the grits are creamy and tender, about 20 minutes.

2. Turn off the heat. Add the cheese and stir until it is completely melted. Season with salt to taste if necessary.

Serves 4

Dry Stout

{ FRENCH ROAST RIBS }

There are a number of varieties of stout, including milk stout, oyster stout and oatmeal stout. But the best-known and most widely consumed style is dry stout. If you've tried Guinness you've tasted the most famous dry stout. All dry stouts are opaque and inky black, a colour achieved through the use of specialty malts. Some brewers will also use a roasted, unmalted barley which gives the desired dark ebony colour and also keeps the head creamy white. While a dry stout may have a very slight aroma of earthy hops, mostly you'll notice the roasted notes of the malt. Aromas of coffee and dark bitter chocolate in all their different forms will predominate, and hiding behind them may be subtle notes of sweet maltiness. Though stouts appear as if they could drink like molasses, they are actually very light in alcohol and weight. The mouthfeel may be creamy if it is served on draught and has been nitrogenated, otherwise it will have a medium mouthfeel with a dry, slightly bitter finish.

PAIRING: *Black Coal Stout,*
Railway City Brewing Co. (Canada)

The dry stout in this pairing is dark and complex, with typical aromas of rich espresso bean and dark bitter cocoa, and a dry stout's characteristic astringency and bitterness on the palate. As with any stout, there is a lot of aroma on offer, in this case veering toward the smokier end of the spectrum, with additional notes of soot, fig, molasses and salty licorice. With medium weight and a gripping mouthfeel, the beer calls for something innately fatty. Pork ribs fit the bill perfectly as their fat makes a nice contrast with the beer's astringency, and their coffee-spiked dry rub mimics the beer's flavours and aromas. These ribs aren't your regular slathered, sweet ribs; they are serious and demand attention. But, just in case you get the urge for some sauciness, I've added a barbecue sauce dip, too. Slow cooking gives the ribs a melting, unctuous texture, which is perfect with the dried leaf, bitter chocolate finish of the stout.

OTHERS TO TRY:
Guinness (Ireland)
Old No. 38 Stout, North Coast Brewing Co. (USA)
Belhaven Black Scottish Stout (Scotland)

{ DRY STOUT }

French Roast Ribs

These addictive ribs get their name from the jolt of java in the rub.

4½ lb (2 kg) pork back ribs

¼ cup (60 mL) dark roast instant coffee

⅓ cup (80 mL) packed brown sugar

2 Tbsp (30 mL) unsweetened cocoa powder

2 Tbsp (30 mL) paprika

1 Tbsp (15 mL) ground cumin

1 Tbsp (15 mL) salt

1 tsp (5 mL) ground cinnamon

½ cup (125 mL) your favourite barbecue sauce

1. Preheat the oven to 325°F (160°C). Cut the pork ribs into manageable pieces, 4 or 5 bones per piece.

2. In a small bowl, stir together the coffee, brown sugar, cocoa powder, paprika, cumin, salt and cinnamon.

3. Lay a piece of heavy duty foil large enough to enclose the ribs on a 17-by-12-inch (43-by-30 cm) rimmed baking sheet. Place the ribs on the foil and sprinkle the coffee mixture all over ribs to coat them completely. Carefully pour ½ cup (125 mL) water onto the foil and wrap the ribs in foil, sealing the edges well (use additional foil if needed to cover the ribs completely).

4. Place the baking sheet on the middle rack of the oven and roast until meat on the ribs is very tender, about 3 hours. If you open the foil during cooking to check if the ribs are done, add another ¼ cup (60 mL) water to the package.

5. When the ribs are cooked, carefully unwrap them and transfer to a serving platter, reserving any cooking juices.

6. In a small bowl, stir together the barbecue sauce and ¼ cup (60 mL) of the reserved cooking juices. Serve the barbecue sauce with the ribs.

Serves 4

FALL

GERMAN PILSENER 128
Cauliflower Soup with Walnut-Parsley Pesto 130

QUADRUPEL 132
Croûtes of Saint Agur, Bacon and Pecans 134

DUNKELWEIZEN 136
Beef, Shitake and Bok Choy Buckwheat Noodles 138

FLANDERS RED 140
Cornish Hen with Bitter Greens, Roasted Grapes and Quinoa 142

ENGLISH PALE ALE 144
Lamb and Sweet Potato Pie 146

BROWN ALE 148
Seared Ribeye with Stilton, Sage and Hazelnut Butter 150

PORTER 152
Braised Sausages with Peppers, Olives and Polenta 154

German Pilsener

{ CAULIFLOWER SOUP *with* WALNUT-PARSLEY PESTO }

German Pilsener (or Pils) is a lager fashioned after the Czech Pilsner style (notice the difference in spelling), first brewed in 1842 with immediate success. In Germany, the style is referred to as Pils, out of respect for its Czech predecessor and to avoid confusion. It is hard to describe the German version without making a comparative reference to the Czech beer that inspired it.

Czech Pilsner (page 72) is brewed with softer water, which makes for a rounder beer with more of a malty sweetness. The German Pils is a leaner version, having a lighter mouthfeel, a more noticeable crispness and more pronounced hop bitterness. As for aroma, you can expect bready notes accented with florality and spice. Neither the malt nor the hops should overwhelm but be harmonious. German Pils has a light, refreshing mouthfeel with a pleasant characteristic bitterness from start to finish.

PAIRING: *Bitburger Premium Pils (Germany)*

When the weather gets chilly, there is nothing like a warm bowl of soup to bring happiness to the table. So, it just made sense to begin the fall chapter with a soup recipe. In general, beer is easier to pair with creamy textured soups than broth-based ones, as creamier soups have the substance and body needed to texturally contrast with the beer. Cauliflower is one of my favourite vegetables for a cream soup as it gives the finished dish a beautiful velvety texture. Add a bit of cream and butter and you have a mouthful of lusciousness.

For creaminess like this we need a beer that delivers some hop bitterness for contrast, which this German Pilsner does. It also provides a good amount of carbonation for scrubbing the palate clean. The aroma and flavour of cauliflower is rather mild so we don't want an overly aromatic beer. Here, the florality of the Pils complements the ground coriander's floral nature, as well as the herbaceousness of the pesto. And the beer's biscuity, melba toast flavour pairs perfectly, acting as a liquid cracker. All of these components make for a simple, yet sophisticated pairing.

OTHERS TO TRY:

Radeberger Pilsner (Germany)
Braumeister Pils, Victory Brewing (USA)
Noble Pils, Samuel Adams (USA)

{ GERMAN PILSENER }

Cauliflower Soup *with* Walnut-Parsley Pesto

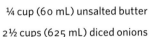

¼ cup (60 mL) unsalted butter

2½ cups (625 mL) diced onions

2 Tbsp (30 mL) coarsely chopped garlic

2 tsp (10 mL) ground coriander

2 Tbsp (30 mL) all-purpose flour

1 medium-sized cauliflower (about 2 lb/1 kg), cut into large florets, stalk and leaves discarded

4 cups (960 mL) vegetable or chicken stock

½ cup (125 mL) coarsely chopped flat-leaf parsley

½ cup (125 mL) walnut halves, lightly toasted and chopped

½ cup (125 mL) olive oil

¼ cup (60 mL) finely grated Parmigiano-Reggiano cheese

½ cup (125 mL) whipping cream (35%)

¼ tsp (1 mL) ground nutmeg

Freshly ground white pepper to taste

Salt to taste

Additional toasted coarsely chopped walnuts for garnish

1. In a large pot, melt the butter over medium heat. Add the onions and cook until softened and translucent, about 15 minutes. Try to avoid browning the onions.

2. Stir in the garlic and coriander and cook, stirring, for 2 minutes. Stir in the flour until it is fully absorbed by the butter.

3. Add the cauliflower, then slowly add the stock plus enough water to come to the top of the cauliflower. Cover the pot and bring to a boil. Reduce the heat to low and simmer until the cauliflower is very tender, about 30 minutes.

4. While the soup is simmering, prepare the pesto by puréeing the parsley, walnuts and olive oil in a blender until smooth. Add the cheese and purée briefly until combined. Scrape the pesto into a small bowl and set aside. Rinse the blender.

5. Once the cauliflower is completely tender (test the thickest pieces with a knife), let the mixture cool slightly then purée it in the blender in batches, if necessary, retuning each batch to the rinsed-out pot. (You can use a hand-held immersion blender but a traditional blender will yield a smoother soup.)

6. Stir the cream, nutmeg, and white pepper to taste into the soup, bring to a simmer over low heat, then simmer for 5 minutes. If the soup is too thick, slowly add a little more water until it is the consistency you like, then simmer for a few minutes more. Season with salt to taste if necessary.

7. Ladle the soup into bowls and serve drizzled with pesto and sprinkled with chopped walnuts.

Serves 6 generously

Quadrupel

{ CROÛTES *of* SAINT AGUR, BACON *and* PECANS }

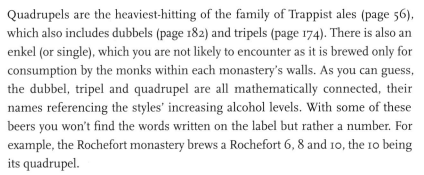

Quadrupels are the heaviest-hitting of the family of Trappist ales (page 56), which also includes dubbels (page 182) and tripels (page 174). There is also an enkel (or single), which you are not likely to encounter as it is brewed only for consumption by the monks within each monastery's walls. As you can guess, the dubbel, tripel and quadrupel are all mathematically connected, their names referencing the styles' increasing alcohol levels. With some of these beers you won't find the words written on the label but rather a number. For example, the Rochefort monastery brews a Rochefort 6, 8 and 10, the 10 being its quadrupel.

One thing you can be sure of with a quadrupel is a high ABV, with some of the strongest ones topping out at 12%. These beers are rich, sweet and strong and offer an abundance of aroma and flavour. You'll smell and taste notes of dark, dried fruits, such as raisin, plum and fig and, depending on the beer, maybe some peppery spice. There also will be rich, complex flavours of brown sugar, nuts, molasses and toffee. The beers have a luscious sweet, round mouthfeel balanced by lavish effervescence.

Outside the monastery walls, the quadrupel is a very popular beer style, and there are plenty of secular breweries throughout the world creating their own versions. Whether Trappist or not, these are big, multifaceted beers that ask to be pondered over. I like to call them meditation beers as they demand your focus and attention. Quadrupels are similar to other strong styles such as imperial stout and barley wine, all very complex beers, that fully express themselves after being allowed time to open up. They are beers to enjoy slowly.

PAIRING: *Rochefort 10,*
Abbaye de Rochefort (Belgium)

The complexity of this dish calls for a beer that has much to offer. These fancy little toasts pack a wallop of flavour and aroma. There are many components to consider—salty, nutty, sweet, smoky and creamy—and you'd think pairing them with a beer so aromatic might create sensory overload. In fact, all of the beer notes are very similar to those in the food. The beer offers gorgeous aromas of buckwheat honey, molasses, licorice, dried dark fruit, pecan tart and toffee, all of which are extremely complementary to the croûtes' flavours.

Texturally, the cheese, bacon and jam all create a luxurious bite of rich sweetness which is cut well by the beer's effervescence. Although high alcohol can sometimes overwhelm a dish that is too delicate, the bold combination of ingredients here has enough substance to stand up to the strength of the beer, making this interesting pairing an overall success.

OTHERS TO TRY:
St. Bernardus Abt 12 (Belgium)
Gulden Draak 9000 Quadruple (Belgium)
Rigor Mortis Abt, Brasserie Dieu du Ciel! (Canada)

{ QUADRUPEL }

Croûtes *of* Saint Agur, Bacon *and* Pecans

8 slices good-quality baguette, sliced 1 inch (2.5 cm) thick

¼ cup (60 mL) unsalted butter

½ cup (125 mL) good-quality black cherry, blueberry, plum or other dark fruit jam

4 slices bacon, cooked and each slice cut into 4 pieces

½ cup (125 mL) pecan halves, toasted and each broken in half again

½ cup (125 mL) dates, pitted and halved

½ cup (125 mL) crumbled Saint Agur or other good-quality creamy blue cheese

1. Position the rack in the top third of the oven and preheat the broiler to high.

2. Butter one side of each baguette slice and place, buttered sides up, on the baking sheet. Broil the baguette slices until lightly golden, watching carefully so they don't burn. Flip the slices and broil until lightly golden on the other side, again watching carefully.

3. Generously spread the buttered side of each toasted baguette slice with jam, then top with equal amounts of bacon, pecans, dates and large crumbles of cheese. Serve at once.

Serves 4 as an appetizer

Dunkelweizen

{ BEEF, SHITAKE *and* BOK CHOY BUCKWHEAT NOODLES }

It would be true to say dunkelweizen (dark wheat) is the big brother to hefe-weizen (page 118). They share the same birthplace—Germany's Bavaria region—and are both excellent partners for food. The beer styles share an easy drinkability and have relatively low alcohol and hopping. Dunkelweizen is brewed with the same bottom-fermenting yeast as the hefeweizen, giving it the enticing aromas of banana and clove that denote the style. Its grain bill includes at least 50% wheat so the beer has a wonderful creamy mouthfeel and persistent mousse-like head. The greatest difference is, of course, the colour. Dunkelweizen is brewed with the addition of dark roasted malts to create a beer that can range from light copper to a dark, transparent chestnut. Along with the yeast's fruit and spice characteristics, there are caramel notes and a light breadiness from the malt. Dunkelweizen is a beer that offers a lot of flavour without fatiguing the palate, and its sweet, malty nature and sparkling effervescence mean it can successfully pair with spicier dishes, which is what I have done here.

PAIRING: *Erdinger Dunkel, Erdinger Weissbräu (Germany)*

I chose a dunkelweizen for this dish because I needed a beer that could multitask. First let's talk weight; both are similar so we're off to a good start. Then we have the beer's high carbonation which is a great partner to the salty nature of the soy-based sauce but also a good textural contrast with the richness of the noodles and meat. The beer's toasted cocoa and bitter browned sugar flavour are ideal complements to the rich meatiness of the soy sauce and shitake mushrooms, as well as the beef. As for taste, this dish abounds in umami—the so-called fifth taste—which accentuates bitter flavours, so the beer needs to be fairly low in bitterness, and lightly hopped dunkelweizen fits the bill. The last task the beer successfully completes is to temper the heat from the chili peppers with the sweetness of its malt. In all, a job well done by this hardworking and versatile beer.

OTHERS TO TRY:

Weihenstephaner Hefeweissbier Dunkel (Germany)
Hacker-Pschorr Dunkel Weisse (Germany)
Dunkelweizen, Smithavens Brewing Company (Canada)

{ DUNKELWEIZEN }

Beef, Shitake *and* Bok Choy Buckwheat Noodles

¼ cup (60 mL) dark soy sauce

3 tsp (15 mL) cornstarch

3 Tbsp (45 mL) vegetable oil

1¼ lb (600 g) inside round, tenderloin or top sirloin, sliced very thinly across the grain

1 Tbsp (15 mL) finely chopped garlic

1 Tbsp (15 mL) peeled and finely chopped fresh ginger

2 tsp (10 mL) finely sliced chili pepper with its seeds (or to taste)

1½ cups (375 mL) thinly sliced shitake mushroom caps (freeze the stems for use in a soup or stock recipe)

1 lb (500 g) baby bok choy, cut in half lengthwise and rinsed

10 oz (300 g) soba buckwheat noodles (can be found where Asian foods are sold)

1 cup (250 mL) thinly sliced green onions, cut on the diagonal

½ cup (125 mL) coarsely chopped cilantro

1 Tbsp (15 mL) toasted sesame oil

1 Tbsp (15 mL) toasted sesame seeds

1. In a small bowl, stir together the soy sauce, cornstarch and ½ cup (125 mL) cold water until the cornstarch has dissolved. Set aside.

2. Bring a large pot of salted water to a boil over high heat.

3. Meanwhile, heat the oil in a large wok or sauté pan over medium-high heat. Add the beef and cook, stirring, until well browned, about 7 minutes.

4. Add the garlic, ginger and chili pepper to the wok and cook, stirring, for 1 minute. Stir in the soy mixture and cook, stirring, for 30 seconds until the sauce has thickened. Remove the beef mixture to a bowl and set aside.

5. Add the mushroom caps and ¼ cup (60 mL) water to the wok. Cook over medium heat for 3 minutes, stirring with a wooden spoon to clean any remaining sauce from the side of the wok.

6. Meanwhile, add the baby bok choy to the large pot of boiling water and blanch for 1 minute. Use a slotted spoon to remove the bok choy from the pot (leave the pot of water boiling) and carefully add them to the wok. Cook, stirring, for 2 minutes.

7. Add the noodles to the pot of boiling water and cook according to the package directions.

8. Meanwhile, return the beef mixture to the wok, along with the green onions. Cook, stirring, until heated through, 2 minutes.

9. Drain the noodles and tip into the wok, along with the cilantro and sesame oil. Toss well to combine the ingredients. Serve garnished with sesame seeds.

Serves 4

Flanders Red

{ CORNISH HEN *with* BITTER GREENS, ROASTED GRAPES *and* QUINOA }

Flanders red originates from the Flanders region in the north of Belgium; more specifically, West Flanders, which is also where Bruges, one of my favourite cities is located. If you love beer, food and beautiful architecture, I urge you to make the trip.

Flanders red is created using a combination of malts to achieve a reddish-brown colour, which is why the beer also goes by the name Flanders red-brown (*roodbruin* in Dutch). And it shouldn't be confused with Flanders brown or *oud bruin* (meaning old brown) which hails from East Flanders and has similar characteristics but is a different beer. One more thing, some call it Flemish red instead of Flanders red. Let's hope that wasn't too confusing!

Flanders red is a sour ale which is spontaneously fermented and sours with a combination of yeast and bacteria. It is left to ferment and age for close to two years in large oak casks called *foudres,* which is when the magic happens. The ale's tart, lactic, funky flavours develop over time and gain additional complexity from the prolonged oak contact, making for an intriguing and complex beer. The sweetness of the malt and the sourness from the effects of Lactobacillus bacteria and Brettanomyces yeast create an enticing sweet-and-sour flavour which is ideal for food pairing. This is a unique beer that is sometimes compared to red wine due to its acidity, complexity and elegance. It is fruity, dry, tart and very interesting and should be searched out if you haven't tried Flanders red, a delicious link to Belgian beer culture and history.

PAIRING: *Cuvée des Jacobins,* *Brouwerij Omer Vander Ghinste (Belgium)*

Usually when creating a beer and food pairing, the food choice comes first then I decide on the beer, but for this pairing, the beer was the conductor of the train. I wanted to pair the sour ale with a dish that was as multifaceted as the beer. The crispy skin and succulent meat of the Cornish hens, and the nutty quinoa are all great at contrasting the sour, acidic component of this Flanders red. I find that goat cheese is always a great partner to beers that have been affected with the funk of Brettanomyces as they share a similar rustic nature, and here the cheese adds some creaminess to harmonize with the tartness. Next, we have the garnish of grapes, plum and dried cranberries, all of

which are links to the bright red fruit characteristics that float from the glass. As a complement to the beer's flavours of dried herb and spice, I have added pink peppercorns, paprika and fresh thyme to the mix to mimic the aromas achieved through aging the beer in oak. A salad of bitter greens slicked with vinaigrette is the final component to this pairing and brings another taste dimension to the plate, adding to the overall interest and elegance.

OTHERS TO TRY:

Rodenbach Grand Cru, Brouwerij Rodenbach (Belgium)
Duchesse de Bourgogne, Brouwerij Verhaeghe (Belgium)
Flanders Red, Forked River Brewing Company (Canada)

{ FLANDERS RED }

Cornish Hen *with* Bitter Greens, Roasted Grapes *and* Quinoa

¼ cup (60 mL) olive oil, divided

1 Tbsp (15 mL) coarsely chopped thyme

1 tsp (5 mL) pink peppercorns, lightly ground with a mortar and pestle or spice grinder

1 tsp (5 mL) paprika

1 tsp (5 mL) packed brown sugar

½ tsp (2 mL) salt, divided

2 Cornish hens (about 1¼ lb/625 g each)

1 cup (250 mL) seedless red grapes

¾ cup (175 mL) quinoa, rinsed and drained

2 Tbsp (30 mL) sherry vinegar or red wine vinegar

2 tsp (10 mL) Dijon mustard

3 cups (720 mL) lightly packed bitter greens, such as dandelion, escarole or arugula, washed, dried and coarsely torn

1 cup (250 mL) coarsely torn radicchio

1 large ripe red plum, pitted and sliced into thin wedges

¼ cup (60 mL) dried cranberries

½ cup (125 mL) crumbled goat cheese

1. In a large bowl, stir together 1 Tbsp (15 mL) olive oil, the thyme, peppercorns, paprika, brown sugar and ¼ tsp (1 mL) salt. Using a very sharp knife or kitchen shears, cut through the breast bone of each Cornish hen, then through the backbones to cut each hen in half. Coat the Cornish hen halves evenly in the thyme mixture. Set aside.

2. Preheat the grill to high and oil the racks. Meanwhile, wrap the grapes in foil and pierce two small holes in the top of the package to release the steam.

3. When the grill is ready, place the Cornish hen halves on the grill, skin sides down. Place the foil package of grapes on the grill next to the Cornish hens. Grill the Cornish hens, without turning, until the skin becomes nicely golden, about 8 minutes. Remove the package of grapes and set aside to cool.

4. Turn off the burner(s) from one side of the grill. Flip the hen halves over and place them over the unlit burner(s), keeping the other side of the grill on high. Close the lid slightly and grill until a meat thermometer inserted in the thickest part of the thighs registers 165°F (75°C). Remove the Cornish hens from the grill and set aside to cool slightly.

5. Meanwhile, stir together 1½ cups (375 mL) water, the quinoa and the remaining salt in a small saucepan. Bring to a boil, then reduce the heat and simmer, covered, until the quinoa is tender, about 15 minutes. Remove from the heat, fluff the quinoa with a fork and set aside.

6. In a large bowl, whisk together the remaining oil, vinegar, mustard and brown sugar. Add the greens, radicchio, plum and cranberries. Season with salt to taste and toss well to combine.

7. Stir the liquid from the package of grapes into the quinoa. Spoon a heaping ½ cup (125 mL) of quinoa on each of four plates. Divide the salad among the plates and top each portion with half a Cornish hen. Garnish with roasted grapes and pieces of goat cheese.

Serves 4

English Pale Ale

{ LAMB *and* SWEET POTATO PIE }

The pale ale style originated in England during the 1700s, and its drinkability, flavour and refreshing hop bitterness make it popular throughout the world. "Pale" references its colour, which is pale only in comparison to the dark beers that predominated in the 18th century. Within this catch-all category, you'll find many different variations of pale ale. The umbrella term covers British ales—or bitters—of varying degrees of alcohol and all with different names: mild, standard ordinary bitter, best bitter, premium bitter and extra special bitter (ESB). The irony is that the term "pale ale" is used more outside England than within.

Though the alcohol levels vary slightly—from 3% to 5.5% ABV—among all these beers, they share common qualities: flavours of toast and caramel, as well as earthy or herbaceous aromas from English hops, and light fruit flavours leaning toward apple and apricot. Their sweet maltiness gives these beers a medium body which is balanced by a clean, pronounced hop bitterness. Overall, they are versatile beers well-suited to being enjoyed on their own or paired with a wide variety of foods.

PAIRING: *Organic Pale Ale,*
Samuel Smith Brewery (England)

Meat in a pie makes me think of British classics, like Cornish pasties, steak and kidney pie, shepherd's pie, the list goes on. Which is why I've chosen to pair a lamb pie with this emblematic British style of beer. The beer's sweet malty nature is perfect with the earthiness of the sweet potato, and its toffee notes are very complementary with the flavour of the golden pastry. The ale's carbonation does a great job of cutting through the richness of the lamb and pastry while the hops give an additional hand at cleansing the palate. The noticeable astringency of the hops also helps to keep things balanced. To link with the beer's fruity nature, I've added dried apricots and the accent of dried spices. The flavour intensity of the pie is somewhat bolder than that of the beer, which works just fine since, rather than compete with all those tastes in the pie, the beer complements them. This is a balanced, flavoursome and thoroughly enjoyable pairing that showcases two English classics.

OTHERS TO TRY:

Pompous Ass, Great Lakes Brewery (Canada)

Fuller's ESB (England)

Geary's Pale Ale, D.L. Geary Brewing Company (USA)

{ ENGLISH PALE ALE }

Lamb *and* Sweet Potato Pie

2 Tbsp (30 mL) vegetable oil

2 cups (500 mL) diced onions

1 cup (250 mL) finely diced celery

2 Tbsp (30 mL) peeled and finely chopped fresh ginger

1 Tbsp (15 mL) finely chopped garlic

2 tsp (10 mL) fennel seeds, lightly crushed

1½ tsp (7 mL) ground cinnamon

1½ tsp (7 mL) salt

1 tsp (5 mL) ground coriander

1¾ lb (875 g) ground lamb

2 Tbsp (30 mL) tomato paste

3 Tbsp (45 mL) all-purpose flour, plus additional for dusting

1 cup (250 mL) pale ale or water

3 cups (720 mL) peeled and diced sweet potato (in 1 inch (2.5 cm) cubes)

1 can (19 oz/540 mL) diced tomatoes with their juices

½ cup (125 mL) coarsely chopped dried apricots

2 bay leaves (optional)

Freshly ground black pepper to taste

1 package (450 g) frozen puff pastry, thawed

1 egg

1 Tbsp (15 mL) milk

1. Preheat the oven to 350°F (180°C).

2. In a large pot, heat the oil over medium-high heat. Add the onions, celery, ginger and garlic, and cook, stirring often, until lightly browned and tender, about 15 minutes. Reduce the heat to low and stir in the fennel seeds, cinnamon, salt and coriander. Cook, stirring, for 30 seconds to toast the spices.

3. Add the lamb and increase the heat to medium-high. Cook, stirring often, until the lamb is lightly browned and the liquid has reduced, about 20 minutes. Add the tomato paste and cook for 3 minutes, stirring to combine it with the other ingredients.

4. Stir in the flour until well combined. Add the ale or water and cook, stirring, for 1 minute.

5. Add the sweet potatoes, tomatoes, apricots, bay leaves and 1 cup (250 mL) water. Bring to a boil over high heat, stir well, then reduce the heat to low. Cover and simmer, stirring occasionally to prevent the mixture from sticking to the bottom of the pot, until the sweet potato is tender and the liquid has almost all evaporated, about 30 minutes. Season the lamb mixture with pepper to taste and more salt, if needed.

6. Meanwhile, dust your work surface with additional flour. Roll out the puff pastry to a square that is at least 1 inch (2.5 cm) larger than the top of a 6- to 7-cup (1.4 to 1.6 L) deep-dish pie plate or baking dish. Invert the empty pie plate on the pastry and, using a sharp knife, cut the pastry 1 inch (2.5 cm) larger than the plate.

7. Place the pie plate on a baking sheet (this will help catch any spills). Using a fork, beat together the egg and milk until very well combined. Brush the edges of the pie plate with this egg wash (this will act as a glue).

8. Pour the lamb mixture into the pie plate. Cover the plate with the puff pastry, crimping the edges so they adhere to the edge of the pie plate.

9. Brush the entire surface of the pastry with egg wash and cut an X in the centre to release the steam. Using the egg wash, you can also glue decorative cut-outs of leftover pastry onto the top of the pie, if desired.

10. Bake the pie until the pastry is golden, about 30 minutes. Let the pie rest for 10 minutes before serving.

Serves 6

Brown Ale

{ SEARED RIBEYE *with* STILTON, SAGE *and* HAZELNUT BUTTER }

Brown ales originated in Britain and fall between pale ales and porters in terms of colour. They enjoyed early success in England but have now gained a very strong foothold with North American craft brewers. Both British and American versions will have a malty sweetness and moderate bitterness, with lovely flavours of caramel, toffee, nuts and chocolate. Hops will be noticeable but balanced and are always in the background compared to the malt. In an American version, you may find the hops more dominant and the beer may also include creative additions, such as nuts, spices or other ingredients to complement its nuttiness. In general, the American versions of brown ale are bolder and more robust than their English counterparts, with higher ABVs, bolder malt profiles and more aggressive hopping.

PAIRING: *Eephus Oatmeal Brown Ale,*
Left Field Brewery (Canada)

The addition of oats to its grain bill gives this American-style brown ale a velvety texture. The beer has wonderful nutty aromas, primarily of pecan, which perfectly complement the notes of hazelnut and the nutty toasted milk solids in the ribeye's butter sauce. Many brown ales include the word "nut" in their name, the term "nut-brown" referring to the beer's colour which is brown like nutshells. But nut-brown works just as well as a descriptor since many of these beers typically have toasted nut flavours.

The texture of this beer is smooth, and the medium- to full-bodied weight is similar to that of the steak. The bitter herbal hop presence is the perfect counterbalance to the decadently rich steak and its sauce. The charring of the steak and the deep toasting of the malt are great partners, adding an abundance of caramelized flavour to each mouthful. Finally, the beer's moderate carbonation and dry finish help to cleanse the palate and entice you back for another bite. This pairing was gulped down on testing day without a streak of sauce left on the plates, or a drop of beer in the glasses—the tasting crew couldn't get enough!

OTHERS TO TRY:

Nut Brown Ale, Samuel Smith Brewery (England)
Hazelnut Brown Nectar, Rogue (USA)
Nut Brown Ale, Black Oak Brewing Co. (Canada)

{ BROWN ALE }

Seared Ribeye *with* Stilton, Sage *and* Hazelnut Butter

Adjust the heat under the skillet when you're searing the steaks to avoid accumulating burnt bits on the bottom of the skillet. The skillet can be a very dark brown, but not black, as any black bits will make the sauce taste burnt. If the skillet does have burnt bits sticking to it after the steaks are cooked, give it a scrub before prepping the sauce.

2 Tbsp (30 mL) olive oil

2 well-marbled boneless rib eye steaks, about 1½ inches (4 cm) thick (1½ lb/750 g each)

Salt and freshly ground black pepper to taste

¼ cup (60 mL) unsalted butter

¼ cup (60 mL) hazelnuts, toasted, skins rubbed off and nuts coarsely chopped

10 sage leaves

½ cup (125 mL) crumbled Stilton or other creamy blue cheese, such as Saint Agur or Roquefort

Wilted spinach and toasted baguette slices to serve

1. In a large, heavy skillet, heat the oil over high heat. Season the steaks generously on both sides with salt and pepper to taste, then carefully place them in the skillet. Cook until browned on one side, about 4 minutes.

2. Flip the steaks and continue to cook until the undersides are nicely browned, about 5 minutes more for medium-rare (a meat thermometer inserted horizontally through the side of the steaks should register 125°F/50°C).

3. Remove the skillet from the heat and set the steaks aside to rest on a cutting board. (See note above if skillet has burnt bits on the bottom.)

4. Discard any excess fat from the skillet and add 3 Tbsp (45 mL) water to it. Place the skillet over medium heat and bring the water to a simmer, stirring to loosen up any browned bits on the bottom of the skillet.

5. Add the butter, hazelnuts and sage leaves and cook until the butter has melted and is golden, and the sage leaves are crispy. Using a fork, whisk the cheese into the butter mixture until it is slightly melted but with a few small chunks remaining.

6. Slicing across the grain, cut the steaks into 1½ inch (4 cm) slices. Divide between two plates and drizzle the butter sauce over the top. Serve with wilted spinach and toasted baguette slices.

Serves 2

Porter

{ BRAISED SAUSAGES *with* PEPPERS, OLIVES *and* POLENTA }

This London-born beer style was named for the hardworking porters who unloaded and delivered goods from ships and barges along the River Thames. Its popularity with these workers eventually led to its being referred to as porter, with a bolder version called a stout porter. In time, the bolder version lost the porter name and became known as stout. And there you have an extremely condensed version of the beginnings of porter and stout.

The two styles share many similarities as they are both brewed with very dark roasted malts which give them their characteristic blackish colour. However, porters tend to be a little lighter in colour and lean toward a maltier profile so, along with the typical coffee and chocolate aromas, you may also detect some caramel or nuttiness. As well, they can have a subtle note of fruitiness from English yeast that shines through, and some earthiness from hops. Porters will have a dry finish but not quite as astringent as that of a stout. They are medium bodied with a creamy, round mouthfeel—the perfect accompaniment to rich, earthy dishes and stewed meats.

PAIRING: *Rascal London Porter,*
Inveralmond Brewery (England)

At the most basic level, this pairing works because beer and sausage have always been wedded together in harmonious bliss; sausages are greasy and beer is carbonated. Of course, they also taste great together, and sausages have for centuries been a culinary mainstay in some of the world's major brewing countries, such as England, Germany and the Czech Republic.

For this pairing I've added a rich sauce to the sausages to layer on a bit more complexity. The porter has delicious dark roasted aromas of chocolate and mocha, and is also earthy and fruity with dark notes of dates and licorice. A complex beer like this needs food with flavour, and the seasoned sausages provide that and then some, while the olives and tomatoes add the touch of umami that links back to the savoury, umami flavours in dark roasted beers such as porter and stout. The rosemary and peppers add a touch of brightness to keep the pairing from getting too dark and heavy. All of this richness is balanced perfectly by the hop's bittersweet chocolate finish that cuts straight through the fat and leaves in its wake a mouthful of scrumptiousness.

OTHERS TO TRY:

Fuller's London Porter (England)
London-Style Porter, Propeller Brewing Co. (Canada)
Porter, Sierra Nevada Brewing Co. (USA)

{ PORTER }

Braised Sausages *with* **Peppers, Olives** *and* **Polenta**

2 Tbsp (30 mL)
olive oil, divided

1½ lb (750 g) mild Italian
sausages (or enough for 4)

2 sweet yellow or orange
peppers, stemmed, seeded and
sliced (about 3 cups/720 mL)

1 Tbsp (15 mL) tomato paste

1 can (14 oz/398 mL) diced
tomatoes with their juice

½ cup (125 mL) Kalamata or
other brined olives, pitted

1 Tbsp (15 mL) coarsely
chopped rosemary

1 cup (250 mL) fine cornmeal

Salt to taste

1. In a large skillet, heat 1 Tbsp (15 mL) oil over medium-high heat. Add the sausages and brown well, about 5 minutes per side. Remove the sausages from the skillet and set aside.

2. Pour the excess fat from the skillet. Add the remaining 1 Tbsp (15 mL) oil to the skillet and reduce the heat to medium. Add the sweet peppers and cook, stirring often, for 5 minutes.

3. Add the tomato paste and cook, stirring, for 1 minute to combine the paste with the peppers. Add the tomatoes, olives, rosemary and ¼ cup (60 mL) water to the skillet and cook for 5 minutes more.

4. Return the sausages to the skillet, along with another ¼ cup (60 mL) water and bring to a boil over high heat. Cover and reduce the heat, then simmer for 25 minutes.

5. Meanwhile, bring 6 cups (1.4 L) water to a boil in a pot over high heat. Slowly whisk in the cornmeal. Immediately reduce the heat to low and stir the cornmeal mixture. Simmer, uncovered and stirring occasionally, until the polenta is thickened, smooth and creamy, about 20 minutes. Season generously with salt.

6. When the sausages are cooked, remove the lid from the skillet and continue cooking, if necessary, until the sauce thickens. Divide the sausages and sauce among four plates and serve with the polenta.

Serves 4

WINTER

BELGIAN STRONG ALE 158
Lobster Risotto with Browned Butter and Roasted Squash 160

SCHWARZBIER 162
Swordfish with Sun-dried Tomatoes, Olives and Balsamic 164

SCOTTISH ALE 166
Maple-Mustard Salmon with Chestnuts, Apple and Brussels Sprouts 168

SAISON 170
Duck Confit with Herbes de Provence 172

TRIPEL 174
Roast Chicken with a Salad of Oyster Mushrooms, Walnuts and Roasted Garlic 176

BALTIC PORTER 178
Soy- and Orange-Braised Short Ribs with Sweet Potatoes 180

DUBBEL 182
Braised Lamb Shanks with Porcini and White Beans 184

BARLEY WINE 186
Braised Pork Shoulder with Cabbage and Apple 188

IMPERIAL STOUT 190
Three-Cheese Toastie with Plum Jam 192

Belgian Strong Ale

{ LOBSTER RISOTTO *with* BROWNED BUTTER *and* ROASTED SQUASH }

This beer style encompasses a wide spectrum of ales. They are a diverse bunch and many of them are so unique, they don't fit neatly into a single box. But it is this diversity that makes Belgium's beer culture so fascinating. Mind you, there are some traits you can be certain to find in the style. Strong ales have complex and intoxicating aromas which circle around fruitiness and a brioche-like maltiness. The Belgian yeast will add some spice, and the ales will be very effervescent. Hop level can vary greatly and the ales live up to their "strong" designation with a precarious level of alcohol that hides itself well within a frothy, medium-weight body.

PAIRING: *Deus Brut des Flandres, Brouwerij Bosteels (Belgium)*

The catch-all category of "golden strong ale" contains some really fascinating beers, and in this pairing, I showcase one of them. Deus Brut des Flandres is brewed as a regular beer but after its first tank fermentation, it goes into Champagne bottles and is left to slowly ferment at cool temperatures to develop its complexity. The ABV is a whopping 11.5% and is elegantly masked behind an incredibly silky texture achieved by its fine bubbles.

With their similar level of sophistication, the beer and food are perfect for each other, but the pairing also succeeds on a technical level. The beer's effervescence gives it enough cleaning power to slice through the persistent creaminess of the rice, butter, roasted squash and lobster. And, when you factor in aromas of both the risotto and the ale, the pairing reaches a euphoric level. The beer's yeast offers an intriguing bouquet, including notes of Muscat, lavender and rosewater which are all wonderful complements to the lobster. The juice and zest of tangerine in the risotto makes for a great link to the orangey Muscat nose, and the hits of sage and Parmigiano-Reggiano are great pops of flavour that mimic the beer's herbal notes of spearmint and thyme. The roasted squash adds an earthy sweetness that complements the round sweet malty body of the beer. And lastly, the persistence and intensity of flavour are equal in a pairing that feels like it was made for royalty.

OTHERS TO TRY:

Delirium Tremens, Brouwerij Huyghe (Belgium)
Maudite, Unibroue (Canada)
Gnomegang, Brewery Ommegang (USA)

Lobster Risotto *with* Browned Butter *and* Roasted Squash

If you prefer, substitute 1 cup (250 mL) cubed lobster meat and 1 cup (250 mL) shelled raw large shrimp for the lobster tails in this decadent risotto.

3 Tbsp (45 mL) olive oil, divided

1 butternut squash (about 1¼ lb/600 g), cut in half lengthwise and seeded

1 cup (250 mL) finely diced onions

2 Tbsp (30 mL) finely chopped garlic

3 Tbsp (45 mL) coarsely chopped sage

¼ cup (60 mL) unsalted butter

1½ cups (375 mL) arborio or carnaroli rice

1 tsp (5 mL) salt

4 cups (960 mL) chicken or vegetable stock, divided

4 small (or 2 large) raw lobster tails (to yield a total of 1½ cups (375 mL) lobster meat)

Finely grated zest and squeezed juice of 1 tangerine or mandarin orange

⅓ cup (80 mL) Parmigiano-Reggiano cheese for garnish

1. Preheat the oven to 350°F (180°C).

2. Oil a glass or metal baking dish, large enough to hold the squash, with 1 tsp (5 mL) olive oil. Place the squash in the dish, cut sides down, and roast, uncovered, until the thickest part is knife-tender, about 1 hour. If needed, add a splash of water to the dish toward the end of the cooking time if the squash looks like it may burn.

3. When cool enough to handle, peel the squash and cut the flesh into cubes (you should have about 2 cups (500 mL); reserve any extra for future use in a soup or stew).

4. In a large pot, heat the remaining olive oil over medium heat. Add the onions and cook, stirring often, until they are translucent, about 10 minutes. Add the garlic and sage and cook, stirring, for 2 minutes more.

5. Add the butter and cook until it melts then begins to brown, but do not let it burn. As soon as the butter is the colour of light toffee or brown sugar, remove the pot from the heat and stir in the rice and salt. Stir the rice to coat it well with the butter; all the grains should shine.

6. Return the pot to medium heat and stir in 2 cups (500 mL) of stock. Add the roasted squash, stir well and bring to a simmer. Let the stock simmer, stirring occasionally to create creaminess and avoid sticking, until the liquid has been absorbed by the rice.

7. Meanwhile, using kitchen shears or sharp knife, cut open the lobster tails starting at the thicker end and moving toward the tail end. Pry the shells open, remove the meat and chop it into 1 inch (2.5 cm) pieces.

8. Once the first 2 cups (500 mL) of stock have been absorbed by the rice, add the remaining stock, along with the tangerine juice. Continue simmering and stirring until the liquid has been absorbed by the rice. At this point, taste a grain of rice to see how cooked it is and whether the risotto needs more salt. The rice should be al dente, meaning it is cooked but still firm and not overly soft. If necessary, add water in ¼ cup (60 mL) increments until the rice is done.

9. During the last few minutes of cooking, stir in the lobster meat and tangerine zest. Cook, stirring often, until the lobster meat is white rather than opaque, about 3 minutes (do not overcook).

10. Divide the risotto among four plates and garnish generously with Parmigiano-Reggiano.

Serves 4

Schwarzbier

{ SWORDFISH *with* SUN-DRIED TOMATOES, OLIVES *and* BALSAMIC }

Schwarzbier is the German word for "black beer," and is a bottom-fermented lager that offers a whole lot of flavour. The term you'll find on the Czech version is *černý*, and you can expect a similar personality. Schwarzbier has the refreshing, clean nature of a lager but with lots of roasted chocolate and coffee notes. I see schwarzbier as having similar traits to Pinot Noir because it has a lightness of body but is not shy on flavour and aroma. Pinot Noir is the go-to red wine for fish, such as salmon, tuna or swordfish, as it doesn't overwhelm their delicate flavours. The same can be said of schwarzbier whose body and mouthfeel are relatively lighter than the aroma it delivers, which means it is perfect for lighter meat dishes and heavier fish, but not so good a match for heartier, meaty foods like braises and stews.

PAIRING: *Köstritzer Schwarzbier (Germany)*

Swordfish—along with salmon, tuna, cod and monkfish— is a "beefier" fish that can accept a lot of flavour without being overwhelmed, and gives this dish substantial weight. One of the biggest considerations here is the sauce. It is full of umami-rich ingredients, such as both fresh and dried tomatoes, balsamic vinegar, and brined olives and capers. The abundance of umami increases the perception of acidity in the beer, which helps to better refresh the palate after a mouthful of the succulent fish and sauce. The perception of the hop bitterness is also elevated by the umami which once again helps to keep this rich dish balanced. The dark savoury nature of the swordfish dish is a great link to the roasted character of the schwarzbier's malt. Also, the malt's sweet roundness gives the beer the body it needs to stand up to all the flavours in the sauce. I really like this combo of food and beer as it showcases how umami works in a pairing, as well as the versatility of beer at the table. In all, it's a real winner.

OTHERS TO TRY:

The Black Lager, Silversmith Brewing Company (Canada)
Mönchshof Schwarzbier, Kulmbacher Brauerei (Germany)
Krušovice Černé (Czech Republic)

{ SCHWARZBIER }

Swordfish *with* Sun-dried Tomatoes, Olives *and* Balsamic

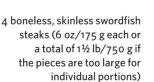

4 boneless, skinless swordfish steaks (6 oz/175 g each or a total of 1½ lb/750 g if the pieces are too large for individual portions)

Salt and freshly ground black pepper to taste

3 Tbsp (45 mL) olive oil, divided

1½ cups (375 mL) cherry tomatoes, halved lengthwise

8 oil-packed sun-dried tomatoes, drained and coarsely chopped

8 Kalamata olives, pitted and coarsely chopped

2 Tbsp (30 mL) drained capers

1 tsp (5 mL) finely chopped thyme

2 Tbsp (30 mL) balsamic vinegar

1 Tbsp (15 mL) coarsely chopped parsley

Additional olive oil for drizzling (optional)

1. Season the swordfish steaks generously with salt and black pepper to taste.

2. Heat 2 Tbsp (30 mL) oil in a large nonstick skillet over medium-high heat. Add the swordfish and cook until golden on one side, about 3 minutes. Carefully turn the steaks over and cook for 2 minutes more. Set aside on a plate (there's no need to cover them).

3. Discard the oil from the skillet. Reduce the heat to medium and add the remaining oil to the skillet. Add the cherry and sun-dried tomatoes, olives, capers and thyme, and cook for 3 minutes, stirring occasionally.

4. Remove the skillet from the heat and add the balsamic vinegar, along with 3 Tbsp (45 mL) water. Stir the mixture to combine.

5. Nestle the swordfish steaks into the tomato mixture, cover the skillet and return it to low heat until the swordfish is cooked through, about 4 minutes. Remove the skillet from the heat and divide the swordfish among four plates. If the sauce seems too thin, return the skillet to the heat and simmer the sauce for a minute longer to thicken it. Stir in the parsley.

6. Top the swordfish with the sauce and drizzle with additional olive oil, if desired.

Serves 4

Scottish Ale

{ MAPLE-MUSTARD SALMON *with* CHESTNUTS, APPLE *and* BRUSSELS SPROUTS }

Scottish ales are the malty pale ales of Scotland and shouldn't be confused with Scotch ales which are altogether heavier, stronger beers. You can expect Scottish ales to have a warm malty nose delivering aromas of rich caramel and occasional nuttiness. They are dry with moderate carbonation and are hopped using a lighter hand compared to English ales. In some of the New World versions of this style, you may find a very light note of smoke similar to that of the smoky peatiness of some scotch. Their alcohol level is relatively low, not venturing much past 5% ABV, and they finish with a pleasing dried herb bitterness which makes them a great choice for food pairing.

PAIRING: *Scottish Ale,*
Highlander Brew Co. (Canada)

One of the most important aspects of this pairing is its bang-on balance between the flavour intensity and weight of both beer and food. The sauce's maple syrup sweetness and mustard acidity and the beer's sweet caramel malt flavour balanced by hops give them similar and complementary personalities. To put it another way: the same but different. Also, the caramelization on the salmon and Brussels sprouts works wonderfully with the rich, toasty caramel flavour of the beer, while the chestnuts echo the beer's delicate nuttiness. The smoky addition of bacon to the dish is a nod to the smoky peat quality that some contemporary Scottish ales share, and adds some richness and great flavour. When looking for cutting properties in the beer we can turn to the moderate carbonation and pleasant astringency of earthy English hops to do the job well. Lastly, aside from flavour and aroma, this is an example of a pairing that makes sense geographically. Salmon is one of Scotland's most revered food items, which makes it a great option for pairing with a Scottish-style beer.

OTHERS TO TRY:

Piper Down Scottish Ale, Ballast Point (USA)
Belhaven Scottish Ale (Scotland)
Farm Table: 80 Shilling, Beau's All Natural Brewing Company (Canada)

{ SCOTTISH ALE }

Maple-Mustard Salmon *with* Chestnuts, Apple *and* Brussels Sprouts

4 slices bacon, cut into 1 inch (2.5 cm) pieces

12 oz (375 g) Brussels sprouts, trimmed and halved lengthwise

1 cup (250 mL) cored and finely diced firm red apple, peel left on (not McIntosh)

½ cup (125 mL) peeled, roasted chestnuts, halved (roasted chestnuts can be found at most grocery stores)

1 tsp (5 mL) finely chopped thyme

¼ cup (60 mL) olive oil, divided

4 salmon steaks (7 oz/200 g each)

Salt and freshly ground black pepper to taste

2 Tbsp (30 mL) grainy mustard

2 Tbsp (30 mL) maple syrup

1. Adjust the oven rack to the middle position and preheat the oven to 400°F (200°C). Bring a medium pot of salted water to a boil.

2. Place the bacon pieces on a large rimmed baking sheet, trying not to overlap them. Cook on the middle rack for 5 minutes.

3. Meanwhile, add the Brussels sprouts to the pot of boiling water and blanch them for 2 minutes. Remove the Brussels sprouts with a slotted spoon and set aside.

4. Remove the baking sheet from the oven and add the Brussels sprouts, apple, chestnuts, thyme and 2 Tbsp (30 mL) olive oil to the bacon. Toss the ingredients together and return the baking sheet to the oven for 20 minutes more.

5. Meanwhile, heat the remaining 2 Tbsp (30 mL) olive oil in a large non-stick skillet over medium heat. Season the salmon steaks with salt and pepper to taste and carefully place in the skillet. Cook until golden on the underside, about 8 minutes. Turn the steaks over and continue cooking until cooked through, about 7 minutes more.

6. While the salmon is cooking, stir together the mustard and maple syrup in a small bowl.

7. When the salmon is ready, pour the maple syrup mixture over the steaks in the skillet. Cook until the maple mixture thickens slightly, about 1 minute.

8. Divide the Brussels sprout mixture among four plates and top each portion with a salmon steak.

Serves 4

Saison

{ DUCK CONFIT *with* HERBES DE PROVENCE }

Saison is one of my favourite beer styles as these beers are super refreshing and have great food compatibility. They were first brewed on farms in the Wallonia region of Belgium, which is why they're also referred to as farmhouse ales. Saison is the French word for "season" and alludes to the time of year these beers were once brewed. Without the luxury of refrigeration, brewers took advantage of the cooler temperatures of fall and winter to brew and store their beers. The beers were made to be ready for the arrival of summer and the area's hired workforce, and were intended to keep farmhands happy and hydrated through the hot months in the fields. Nowadays, saisons are brewed all year round. Even though it is still considered a summertime beer, I feel saisons have a place at the table in any season so have paired this style with a comforting winter dish of duck confit.

Saisons are beers with great effervescence, a dry mouthfeel and a pleasingly bitter finish. They are highly aromatic, with fruity yeast aromas reminiscent of orange and lemon, and a subtle pepperiness. The grains used for saisons can vary and are usually a combination of barley, along with wheat, oats and/or rye, all giving their own personality to the beer. The act of blending different cereal grains echoes back to the time when farmers would use surplus grain when making their beer, which meant the recipe could change annually depending on what was left at the end of the season. The malt character of the beer can be grain-like, with a spiciness from rye or wheat. The hops used can offer different aromas depending on the variety used, and their astringency will be noticeable. Sometimes spices, such as coriander or grains of paradise, are included for interest and, in some contemporary versions, there may also be the addition of fruit.

PAIRING: *Saison Dupont, Brasserie Dupont (Belgium)*

This is a classic version of saison, and I chose to pair it with duck confit as the two are made for each other. Both beer and food are equal in weight and complexity, and have a similar intensity of flavour. The elegant dry nature of the beer is the perfect match for the innate richness and fattiness of duck confit, drying the palate off for the next succulent bite. Its spicy, lemony aroma is a great link with the combination of complementary aromatics used in the herbes de Provence blend, which includes dried thyme, rosemary and lavender. Both the dish and beer are equally fragrant and enticing.

Duck confit runs the risk of inundating the palate with fattiness but the saison's hop bitterness saves this from happening by keeping things harmonious and balanced and, of course, its lively effervescence is refreshing. The success of this pairing is apparent when you notice the beer still manages to retain its elegance and flavour even up against the bold richness of the duck. And when the beer and duck are enjoyed together, the taste experience is elevated beyond the pleasure each provides individually. Bon appetit!

OTHERS TO TRY:
St-Feuillien Saison (Belgium)
Sofie, Goose Island Beer Co. (USA)
La Saison du Tracteur, Le Trou du Diable (Canada)

{ SAISON }

Duck Confit *with* Herbes de Provence

I like kosher salt for this recipe as its larger crystals work perfectly to slightly cure the duck legs before cooking.

1 Tbsp (15 mL) whole rosemary leaves

1 tsp (5 mL) dried herbes de Provence (or a mixture of dried thyme, rosemary and/or lavender)

1 tsp (5 mL) kosher salt

½ tsp (2 mL) freshly ground black pepper

2 bay leaves, broken into large pieces

4 duck legs (2¼ lb /1.1 kg total weight)

1 tsp (5 mL) olive oil

Mashed potatoes and sautéed Swiss chard or spinach to serve

1. In a glass baking dish large enough to hold the duck legs in one layer, mix together the rosemary, herbes de Provence, salt, black pepper and bay leaves.

2. Pat the duck legs dry with paper towel. Lightly season the flesh side of the duck legs with some of the herb mixture, then place them, skin side down, in the dish. Cover with plastic wrap and refrigerate for 18 to 24 hours.

3. The next day, wipe off all the herb mixture. With a sharp knife, score the skin of the duck legs without cutting through into the meat.

4. Preheat the oven to 300°F (150°C). In a large ovenproof skillet, heat the olive oil over medium-low heat. Add the duck legs, skin side down, and cook until the duck legs have rendered some of their fat, about 20 minutes.

5. Turn the duck legs over. Standing back in case the fat splatters, add ¼ cup (60 mL) water to the skillet. Cover the skillet with a lid or foil and cook in the oven for 2½ hours.

6. Uncover the skillet and continue to cook in the oven until the skin of the duck legs is crisp and brown, about 20 minutes more.

7. Divide the duck legs among four plates (reserve the duck fat for another use, such as roast potatoes). Serve the duck confit with mashed potatoes and sautéed Swiss chard or spinach.

Serves 4

Tripel

{ ROAST CHICKEN *with a* SALAD OF OYSTER MUSHROOMS, WALNUTS *and* ROASTED GARLIC }

Belgian tripel, is part of the Trappist family of beers, which includes dubbel (page 182) and quadrupel (page 132). Tripel sits in between these two and is the only golden-coloured beer of the three. This tends to lead to confusion as its lighter hue implies that, of the three styles, tripel would be mildest in flavour and lowest in alcohol, but this is not true. Its alcohol can range from 7 to 10% ABV and the beer is loaded with flavour. You can expect a lot of complexity derived from the yeasts used, which give fruity notes of banana, orange and lemon zest, and spicy notes of pepper. Tripels are typically bottle-conditioned which means there will be an exuberant amount of bubbles and a medium, round mouthfeel. The use of hops is evident and the beers will reveal bitterness on the palate and in the drying finish. Carbonation, alcohol and bitterness are all bold, but there is an equal amount of fruity personality, sweet malt and spiciness to keep these wonderfully food-friendly beers balanced.

PAIRING: *Tripel Karmeliet, Brouwerij Bosteels (Belgium)*

This abbey ale is brewed with a combination of three grains—barley, wheat and oats. Tripels are typically brewed with barley only, but this version references back to an old Brouwerij Bosteels recipe. Even with the additional grains, the ale stays within the parameters of a traditional tripel. The addition of wheat gives it an ethereal lightness and the oats augment the already creamy, smooth mouthfeel. The aromas presented by the beer are exotic and enticing: banana and warm citrus notes, honey and fragrant white flowers. All these are great complements to the rich, warm flavours of the chicken. First, its sweet caramelized skin has a very similar personality to the caramelized notes of the malt. The chicken's oiliness is cleaned away by the beer's frothy effervescence, as well as by the cleansing nature of the hops. The chicken on its own would lack the interest to match the wealth of flavour and mouthfeel of a tripel. But add in earthy mushrooms, crispy sage, sweet roasted garlic and the bitterness of walnuts and you've brought it to a place where all the stars align.

OTHERS TO TRY:

St. Bernardus Tripel, Brouwerij St. Bernardus (Belgium)
La Trappe Tripel, Brouwerij de Koningshoeven (Belgium)
Gouden Carolus Tripel, Brouwerij Het Anker (Belgium)

{ TRIPEL }

Roast Chicken *with a* Salad *of* Oyster Mushrooms, Walnuts *and* Roasted Garlic

1 chicken (3 ½ lb/1.6 kg)

Salt and freshly ground black pepper to taste

¼ cup (60 mL) unsalted butter, softened

10 sage leaves, divided

3 Tbsp (45 mL) olive oil

10 cloves garlic, unpeeled

2 cups (500 mL) trimmed and sliced oyster mushrooms (in 1 inch/2.5 cm slices)

6 cups (1.4 L) lightly packed, washed and dried arugula

⅓ cup (80 mL) walnut halves, lightly toasted and coarsely chopped

1. Preheat the oven to 425°F (220°C).

2. Generously season the chicken inside and out with salt and pepper. Using kitchen twine, tie the chicken's legs together. Rub the exterior of the chicken with butter and dot with five of the sage leaves.

3. Drizzle the olive oil in a roasting pan, then place chicken in the pan, breast side up, along with the garlic cloves. Roast, uncovered, for 30 minutes.

4. Carefully add the mushrooms and remaining sage leaves to the pan. Sprinkle them with salt and stir to coat with the oil in the pan. Baste the chicken with the pan juices to moisten it, then return the pan to the oven and roast until a meat thermometer placed between the breast and leg, but not touching any bones, registers 165°F (75°C) and the juices run clear when the chicken is pierced with a knife, about 30 minutes more.

5. Remove the chicken to a cutting board and let rest for 5 minutes. Spread the arugula out on a serving platter and top with the mushrooms, roasted garlic and walnuts, then place the chicken on top and drizzle with the pan juices. Carve the chicken into pieces and serve with the salad.

Serves 4

Baltic Porter

{ SOY- *and* ORANGE-BRAISED SHORT RIBS *with* SWEET POTATOES }

Baltic porters are very interesting and unique beers with the same deep, dark colour and aromas of a porter. Their roots are in England where they were first brewed for export to Russia as ales. Over the years, those English roots replanted themselves in Russia and the surrounding Baltic countries, and breweries there began brewing the porters using lager yeast rather than the ale yeast more typically used in porter. The roots grew so deeply that, today, Poland, Germany and, of course, Russia are the primary brewers of the style.

Baltic porters were built for the frigid weather of Europe's northern nations where high alcohol is well-regarded and believed to have the ability to keep people warm over the cold winter months. The beers range from about 5 to 10% ABV. They are sweet, rich and malty with the bittering effects coming from the dark roasted malt, which also provides aromas and flavours of caramel, dark fruit, coffee, chocolate, nuts and a dark, licoricey note of molasses.

PAIRING: *Baltic Porter,*
Smuttynose Brewing Company (USA)

When I think of pairings for very dark roasted, full-flavoured beers, such as porters and stouts, I think of beef or lamb. The dark, coffee-like aromas and meaty nature of these beers are great partners to flavourful, well-marbled cuts of meat, and they typically have the structure needed to stand up to the unctuous, rich effects of braising. Braised beef short ribs have a richness and persistence of flavour which matches perfectly with the hefty weight, high alcohol and deep roasted coffee notes of the Baltic porter. Dark roasted beers such as this have the savoury taste of umami which links it perfectly to the umami-packed soy in the sauce. The sweet potatoes add body to the dish, as well as an earthiness that goes beautifully with the herbaceous nature of the hops. To help cut the richness, we have the coffee and bittersweet chocolate astringency of the dark malt with some added help from the hops. Both the beer and the dish have similar personalities in that they are luxurious, deep, complex, and warming for the soul.

OTHERS TO TRY:

Porter Baltique, Microbrasserie Les Trois Mousquetaires (Canada)
Baltika 6 Porter, Baltika Breweries (Russia)
Żywiec Porter (Poland)

{ BALTIC PORTER }

Soy- *and* Orange-Braised Short Ribs *with* Sweet Potatoes

4½ lb (2 kg) beef short ribs, cut into 2-rib pieces

Salt and freshly ground black pepper to taste

2 Tbsp (30 mL) vegetable oil

2 cups (500 mL) finely chopped onions

1 cup (250 mL) finely chopped celery

2 Tbsp (30 mL) finely chopped garlic

1 Tbsp (15 mL) peeled and finely chopped fresh ginger

3 Tbsp (45 mL) tomato paste

1 tsp (5 mL) chili flakes

4 cups (960 mL) beef stock

½ cup (125 mL) orange juice

⅓ cup (80 mL) soy sauce

3 lb (1.5 kg) sweet potatoes, peeled and coarsely chopped

¼ cup (60 mL) unsalted butter

¼ cup (60 mL) whipping cream (35%) or sour cream

3 tsp (15 mL) cornstarch

½ cup (125 mL) thinly sliced green onions

1. Adjust the oven rack to the middle position and preheat the oven to 325°F (160°C).

2. Season the ribs generously with salt and pepper. In a large pot, heat the oil over medium-high heat. Brown the ribs on all sides, about 5 minutes per side. Work in batches so as not to overcrowd the pot, and add more oil, if needed, to prevent scorching. As each batch is browned, transfer the ribs to a large roasting pan.

3. Pour off all but 1 Tbsp (15 mL) oil from the pot. Reduce the heat to medium and add the onions, celery, garlic and ginger. Cook, stirring often, until the vegetables are tender, about 15 minutes. Add the tomato paste and chili flakes, and cook, stirring, for 1 minute.

4. Add the beef stock, orange juice and soy sauce to the pot. Bring just to a boil, then pour the mixture over the ribs. If needed, add enough water so the liquid comes one-third of the way up the meat. Cover the pan tightly with foil and place on the middle rack of the oven. Cook for 1 hour, then carefully turn the ribs over. Recover the pan with the foil, then cook until the meat is very tender and beginning to fall off the bones, 1½ hours more.

5. While the ribs are cooking, place the sweet potatoes in a large pot and add enough water to come 2 inches (5 cm) above the potatoes. Bring to a boil over high heat, then reduce the heat to low and cook, covered, until the sweet potatoes are fork tender, about 15 minutes. Strain and return the sweet potatoes to the pot. Add the butter and cream and mash coarsely with a potato masher or wooden spoon. Season with salt to taste and keep warm.

6. Once the ribs are cooked, carefully strain the cooking liquid through a sieve into a small saucepan (you should have about 2 cups (500 mL) of cooking liquid). Discard all but 1 cup (250 mL) of the vegetable mixture from the roasting pan. Turn off the oven. Recover the roasting pan with foil and return it to the oven to keep warm.

7. In a small bowl, stir together the cornstarch and ¼ cup (60 mL) water until the cornstarch has dissolved. Add the mixture to the cooking liquid in the saucepan, along with the reserved vegetable mixture. Cook over medium-high heat until the sauce has thickened slightly, about 2 minutes. If needed, let the sauce simmer until it reduces to the right consistency. Season with salt and pepper to taste, if needed.

8. Divide the ribs, sweet potatoes and sauce among four plates and serve garnished with green onions.

Serves 4

Dubbel

{ BRAISED LAMB SHANKS *with* PORCINI *and* WHITE BEANS }

Years before I became interested in beer, my beverage choices centred around the world of wine. I would enjoy the occasional beer but that usually meant a pale lager at a backyard barbecue, or perhaps a Guinness if I was trying to get into the Irish spirit. Then one day I tasted the iconic Westmalle Dubbel. I didn't know much about the beer then, but felt I'd experienced a conscious awakening. The dubbel made me realize there was far more to the world of beer. That one beer sparked a fire in me to learn all I could about the world's different beers, an endeavour that seems to have no end, as the information available could take a lifetime to digest. But I digress; let us get back to dubbel.

This is the dark mahogany, red-hued, hazy brother of the Trappist tripel (page 174) and quadrupel (page 132). A warming and well-hidden alcohol level ranging between 6 and 8% makes dubbel the least strong of the three. Dubbels are rich in their maltiness and can offer luscious aromas and flavours of caramel and cocoa, and a toastiness similar to raisin bread. The dark fruity notes are those of prunes, raisins and black cherries, and there may also be a subtle note of spice or pepperiness. Lastly, these Trappist ales are bottle-conditioned which means they are imbued with a lively effervescence making them great for food pairing. Dubbel is a Trappist-style ale but is also produced by many secular breweries, and will sometimes go by the name *bruin* or *brune* (respectively, Flemish and French for "brown").

PAIRING: *Westmalle Dubbel,*
Brouwerij der Trappisten van Westmalle (Belgium)

At the risk of sounding corny, the depth of malty richness in this Trappist-style beer is heavenly. It is so full of flavour, I've chosen it as the pairing for an equally flavourful braised lamb. The beer and lamb have a similar mouth-feel, weight and persistency. The earthiness of the mushrooms and beans is complemented perfectly by the rich toasted notes of the malt, which gives complementary notes of milk chocolate and cappuccino. The beer's substantial body and alcohol give it enough weight to not be lost behind the braised

lamb and velvety beans. But, the most important component of the beer's pairing potential is its carbonation. Since the beer's hop character is relatively low, we must rely on carbonation to clean the palate. Fortunately, dubbels are bottle-conditioned meaning they deliver a wealth of lively effervescence making them more than up to the task of cutting through this unctuous and saucy dish.

OTHERS TO TRY:
Chimay Red (Belgium)
Dominus Vobiscum Lupulus, Microbrasserie Charlevoix (Canada)
Maredsous 8 Bruin, Duvel Moortgat (Belgium)

{ DUBBEL }

Braised Lamb Shanks *with* **Porcini** *and* **White Beans**

⅓ cup (80 mL) dried porcini mushrooms

4 lamb shanks (about 1 lb/500 g each)

Salt and freshly ground black pepper to taste

3 Tbsp (45 mL) olive oil

2 cups (500 mL) finely chopped onions

3 Tbsp (45 mL) coarsely chopped garlic

2 Tbsp (30 mL) coarsely chopped sage

2 Tbsp (30 mL) tomato paste

4 cups (960 mL) beef stock or water

1 bay leaf

2 cans (19 oz/540 mL each) white, navy or cannellini beans, drained and rinsed

1. Preheat the oven to 325°F (160°C).

2. In a small bowl, combine the mushrooms with 1 cup (250 mL) boiling water, and let rehydrate for 20 minutes.

3. Season the shanks generously with salt and pepper. In a large pot or Dutch oven, heat the oil over medium-high heat. Add the lamb shanks and brown well on all sides, about 20 minutes. Work in batches if necessary to avoid overcrowding the pot. As each batch is browned, transfer the lamb shanks to a large roasting pan.

4. Discard all but 1 Tbsp (15 mL) of oil from the pot. Reduce the heat to medium and add the onions, garlic and sage. Cook, stirring often, until the onions are tender, about 15 minutes. Add the tomato paste and cook, stirring, 1 minute more.

5. Remove the mushrooms from the soaking liquid. Strain the soaking liquid through a fine sieve and reserve. Coarsely chop the mushrooms, then add to the pot, along with their soaking liquid, the stock and bay leaf.

6. Bring the contents of the pot to a gentle boil over high heat, then pour the entire mixture over the lamb shanks. Cover the roasting pan tightly with foil and cook in the oven for 1½ hours.

7. Carefully turn the shanks over. Add the beans to the roasting pan, along with enough water, if needed, to just cover the beans. Recover the pan with foil and return it to the oven until the lamb shanks are very tender and the meat is falling off the bones, 1½ hours more.

8. If there is too much liquid in the pan once the lamb shanks are done, continue to cook a while longer without the foil until the liquid reduces and thickens. Season with salt and pepper to taste. Divide the lamb shanks and beans among four plates.

Serves 4

Barley Wine

{ BRAISED PORK SHOULDER *with* CABBAGE *and* APPLE }

Barley wine is named for its elevated alcohol level of 9 to 13% ABV, which is similar to that of wine. It is a strong, top-fermented ale with loads of delicious dried fruit aromas, such as figs, raisins and prunes. It can have aromas of caramel or toffee which are reminiscent of British sticky puddings, and some will display a nutty sherry-like note. Barley wine has a full-bodied mouthfeel on account of the viscous, warming alcohol and malty sweetness. Hopping can vary depending on whether it is an American or British barley wine, the latter showing less hop character than the former. Barley wines are labours of love as they are rather time-intensive and costly to produce, which makes them all the more revered. Barley wines will sometimes be labelled with a vintage date stating the year of production, because this is a beer style that takes well to aging and can become a beguiling indulgence with a little time behind it.

PAIRING: *Woolly Bugger Barley Wine,*
Howe Sound Brewing (Canada)

The luscious braised pork dish is a complementary pairing for barley wine and worthy of accompanying such a special beer style. First there is the toffee-sweet maltiness of the barley wine that is quite similar to the caramelization that occurs when the pork is darkly seared at the beginning of the recipe. This caramelized crust dissolves as the pork is braised, bringing caramel notes to the sauce. One of the secret ingredients that really helps bridge the flavours in the pairing is the addition of dates to the pork, which melt into the sauce as they slowly cook. The sweet, treacly dates and apple both add a sweetness to the sauce that complements the beer's malty and fruity nature. And the innate succulence of pork shoulder adds richness which is capable of standing up to the beer's fiery 10% ABV. To avoid having too much sweetness in the dish, the cabbage acts as a counterbalance, and grainy mustard is stirred into the sauce at the last moment for a hint of acidity and tang to keep the pairing balanced and harmonious. Enjoy!

OTHERS TO TRY:
Old Foghorn Ale, Anchor Brewing (USA)
J.W. Lees Harvest Ale (England)
Solstice d'hiver, Brasserie Dieu du Ciel! (Canada)

{ BARLEY WINE }

Braised Pork Shoulder *with* Cabbage *and* Apple

2¾ lb (1.25 kg) boneless pork shoulder (also called butt)

Salt and freshly ground black pepper to taste

5 Tbsp (75 mL) vegetable oil, divided

4 cups (960 mL) coarsely chopped onions, divided

1 cup (250 mL) coarsely chopped celery

5 cloves garlic, coarsely chopped

2 tsp (10 mL) paprika

2 tsp (10 mL) fennel seeds

2 tsp (10 mL) coarsely chopped rosemary

¼ cup (60 mL) chopped pitted dates

8 cups (2 L) coarsely chopped Savoy cabbage

1 red apple, cored and finely chopped, peel left on (not McIntosh)

¼ cup (60 mL) whipping cream (35%)

2 Tbsp (30 mL) grainy Dijon mustard

1. Preheat the oven to 300°F (150°C).

2. Season the pork generously with salt and pepper. In a large ovenproof pot, heat 3 Tbsp (45 mL) oil over medium-high heat. Brown the pork until deep golden on all sides, about 5 minutes per side. Remove the pork from pot and set aside.

3. Discard all but 1 Tbsp (15 mL) oil from the pot. Reduce the heat to medium and add 3 cups (720 mL) onions, the celery and garlic to the pot. Cook, stirring often, until the onions are translucent, 10 minutes. Add the paprika, fennel seeds and rosemary, and cook, stirring, for 1 minute.

4. Return the pork to the pot, along with the dates and 2 cups (500 mL) of water. Bring to a boil, cover and place in the oven. Cook for 2½ hours, making sure to turn the pork over halfway through cooking time.

5. While the pork is cooking, heat the remaining 2 Tbsp (30 mL) vegetable oil in a second large pot over medium-high heat. Add the remaining 1 cup (250 mL) onions and cook until tender, about 15 minutes.

6. Add the cabbage, apple and ½ cup (125 mL) water. Cover and cook until cabbage is tender, about 20 minutes. Remove the lid and continue cooking until the liquid has reduced. Set the cabbage aside until ready to serve.

7. When pork is cooked, carefully remove it from the pot. Using a sieve, strain the cooking liquid into a medium bowl, making sure to push down on the solids to extract all the flavour and liquid.

8. Return the pork and strained cooking liquid to the pot, along with the cream and mustard. Simmer over medium heat until the liquid has reduced and reached a sauce-like consistency, 5 to 10 minutes, depending on how much liquid there is left in the pot.

9. Remove the pork from the pot, slice it into four portions and divide it among four plates. Season the sauce with salt and pepper to taste, if necessary. Serve the pork with the sauce and cabbage.

Serves 4

Imperial Stout

{ THREE-CHEESE TOASTIE *with* PLUM JAM }

Imperial stout is one of the boldest and most complex beer styles. If you open one, you'll want to pull up a chair and stay awhile. The term "imperial" refers not only to its high alcohol content, which ranges from 8 to 12% ABV, but also to its origins: the beer was first brewed in England for export to the nobility of the Russian court. The wealthy aristocrats believed stronger meant better, so the beer was brewed to intoxicating levels. It became a grand success and was dubbed Russian imperial stout. Nowadays many craft brewers have at least one imperial stout in their lineup for when the wintry weather hits.

The beer is dark brown to black, and offers loads of aromas of dried dark fruit, roasted nuts, roasted coffee and chocolate and with, usually, a wealth of other notes, too. Hop character will be dictated by whether the hops are American or British. Imperial stout is often aged in repurposed bourbon barrels, which will also deliver some alluring notes of vanilla and spice. The beer has a large, full, round mouthfeel, which is amplified by its fiery alcohol content. In addition, there should be a pronounced bitterness to keep any sweetness in check.

PAIRING: *KBS (Kentucky Breakfast Stout), Founders Brewing Co. (USA)*

When pairing food with an enormous beer like this one, you need to keep certain considerations in mind. Imperial stouts are rich, complex and powerful, and sweet and persistent in their flavour so I suggest not choosing a dish that is overly complex or there will be too much confusion in the mouth. But, what you do need is something substantial enough to be able to stand up to all that personality in the beer. For this pairing, I looked for a dish with the weight and persistence to confront the beer. This super-rich cheese toastie is the perfect partner. The buttery richness of the trio of flavour-packed cheeses

gives it all the tactile attributes we need for the beer. Good-quality cheese is a great companion for beer and the ones in the toastie are rich and dense in texture and flavour. They also have a high fat content which is needed to temper the heat of the alcohol. The sweetness in both the stout and the plum jam are complementary, and the jam also works as a flavour builder for the sandwich and echoes the plummy dried fruit aromas of the beer. Spread the jam in the sandwich and don't hesitate to smear some extra on each bite as it is an integral part of this pairing.

OTHERS TO TRY:

Eldon Imperial Stout, Thornbridge Brewery (England)
Ten Fidy, Oskar Blues Brewery (USA)
Kentucky Bastard, Nickel Brook Brewing Co. (Canada)

{ IMPERIAL STOUT }

Three-Cheese Toastie *with* Plum Jam

8 slices bread (¾ inch/ 2 cm thick), cut from a good-quality loaf of dense bread

1 cup (250 mL) plum jam

4 oz (125 g) creamy blue cheese, such as Gorgonzola, Saint Agur or Roquefort, crumbled

4 oz (125 g) Taleggio or fontina, grated

4 oz (125 g) alpine cheese, such as Gruyère, Beaufort or Emmenthal, grated

¼ cup (60 mL) softened salted butter (or more to taste)

1. Place 4 slices of bread on your work surface and generously smear each with plum jam.

2. Divide all the cheeses evenly among the jam-covered slices.

3. Top the cheese with remaining slices of bread. Generously butter the top side of the toasties.

4. Heat a large skillet over medium heat and place the toasties, buttered sides down, in the skillet. Now carefully butter the top sides of the toasties. (If your skillet isn't large enough to accommodate all the toasties at once, cook them in batches.)

5. Cook the toasties until they are golden on the undersides and the cheese has begun to melt, about 5 minutes.

6. Flip the toasties and cook until golden on second side and the cheese has melted, about 5 minutes more. Let cool slightly, then cut in half and serve with additional plum jam.

Serves 4

ACKNOWLEDGMENTS

I would first like to thank my friend and brilliant photographer Leonardo Frusteri who has always been incredibly generous with his advice and time. Without his talent, the book would not be as beautiful as it is. *Sei un grande, Leo. Grazie di tutto.*

I would also like to recognize the beer writers who have created a foundation of information from which we can all learn. They did the hard work first. Long before the Internet, they were putting pen to paper to gather the material we so easily access today. Respect and appreciation go out to Michael Jackson, Randy Mosher, Roger Protz, Garrett Oliver and Stephen Beaumont, as well as all the other writers who have learned then shared.

Two very important people I'd like to thank are Julia Aitken, for her patience, guidance and intelligence while editing the manuscript, and art director Andrew Bagatella, for his sophisticated eye and the delightful manner which made him such a pleasure to work with. These two people were instrumental in bringing this book to fruition.

A great deal of gratitude goes out to Monda Rosenberg, Tracy Bordian, Denise Schon, Sharon Fitzhenry and Nick Rundall, all of whom have been generous with their good vibes, open hearts and knowledgeable advice and direction.

Tommy, Mom, Max and Georgia, thank you for being patient throughout the writing of this book. It's all done now and you can have me back. XO.

IMAGE CREDITS

All photos in this book were taken by Leonardo Frusteri of Studio Blu in Toronto, Canada, unless mentioned below.

Pg 1: Jon Tyson on Unsplash (sign)

Pg 4: Markus Spiske on Unsplash (hops)

Pg 5: Kiki Pertiñez on Pixabay (malt bags)/PublicDomainPictures on Pixabay (barley)

Pg 6: PublicDomainPictures on Pixabay (water)

Pg 7: Rita Eisenkolb (hops) on Pixabay/ Samuel Smith Brewery (brew kettle)

Pg 8: Budějovický Budvar (testing beer)

Pg 10: Neha Deshmukh (cherries) on Unsplash/Gokalp Iscan on Pixabay (coriander)

Pg 11: Nathan Dumlao www. nathandumlaocreative.com (coffee beans)

Pg 16: Anheuser-Busch (kegs)

Pg 19: Founders Brewing (barrel)

Pg 20: PublicDomainPics on Pixabay (beer)

Pg 22: Peter Kraayvanger on Pixabay (beer glasses on tray)

Pg 24: Daria Yakovleva on Pixabay (bread)

Pg 26: Brouwerij Westmalle

Pg 28: Benjamin Balazs on Pixabay (hay bales)

Pg 29: Anheuser-Busch (beer)

Pg 30: Ernesto Rodriquez on Pixabay (beer)

Pg 31: Founders Brewing (barrel)

Pg 32: Todd Quackenbush on Unsplash

Pg 34: Christiann Koepke on Unsplash (dessert)

Pg 35: David Kaspar (radicchio) on Pixabay/Peter Chou (lemon)

Pg 36: Rupert Kittinger-Sereinig on Pixabay (salt)/Tommaso Cantelli on Unsplash (oysters)

Pg 37: Markus Spiske on Pixabay (tomato paste)/Christine Siracusa on Unsplash (mushrooms)

Pg 38: Aline Ponce on Pixabay (butter)/ Thomas Ulrich on Pixabay (garlic)

Pg 39: Andreas Lischka on Pixabay (peppers)

Pg 49: Jack Harner on Unsplash (beer)

Pg 53: Adam Wilson on Unsplash (bottles)

Pg 57: Orval Brewery

Pg 61: Lindemans Brewery

Pg 73: Vigan Hajdari on Pixabay (draught)

Pg 81: Jonas Jacobsson on Pixabay (beer)

Pg 87: Micheile Henderson on Unsplash (bar)

Pg 95: Abigail Miller on Unsplash (cherry tree)

Pg 99: Quentin DR on Unsplash (cheers)

Pg 103: Alexandra alexas_fotos on Pixabay (beer stein)

Pg 107: Brigitte Tohm on Unsplash (apricots)

Pg 111: Marcelo Ikeda Tchelão on Pixabay (draught)

Pg 115: Brigitte Tohm on Unsplash (wood)

Pg 129: Raphael Rychetsky on Unsplash (barley)

Pg 133: Rochefort Brewery (brew kettles)

Pg 137: Rita Eisenkolb on Pixabay (hops)

Pg 141: Brouwerij Omer Vander Ghinste (foeders)

Pg 145: Kyle Wagner on Unsplash (man)

Pg 149: Adam Wilson on Unsplash (bottles)

Pg 153: Peter Holmes on Pixabay (brewery)

Pg 159: Fabio Neo Amato on Unsplash (brasserie)

Pg 163: A. Bruelmann on Pixabay (bottles)

Pg 167: Ariana Prestes on Unsplash (sheep)

Pg 171: Brasserie Dupont

Pg 179: CongerDesign on Pixabay (winter)

Pg 183: Brouwerij der Trappisten van Westmalle

Pg 187: Yutacar on Unsplash (cheers)

Pg 191: Ethan Weil on Unsplash (barrels)

INDEX